T0131633

Also by Daniel Mitel

THIS NOW IS ETERNITY

HEART IMAGERY

A Path to Enlightenment

DANIEL MITEL

BALBOA.
PRESS
A DIVISION OF HAY HOUSE

Balboa Press books may be ordered through booksellers or by contacting:

Balboa Press
A Division of Hay House
1663 Liberty Drive
Bloomington, IN 47403
www.balboapress.com
1 (877) 407-4847

Because of the dynamic nature of the Internet, any web addresses or links contained in this book may have changed since publication and may no longer be valid. The views expressed in this work are solely those of the author and do not necessarily reflect the views of the publisher, and the publisher hereby disclaims any responsibility for them.

The author of this book does not dispense medical advice or prescribe the use of any technique as a form of treatment for physical, emotional, or medical problems without the advice of a physician, either directly or indirectly. The intent of the author is only to offer information of a general nature to help you in your quest for emotional and spiritual well-being. In the event you use any of the information in this book for yourself, which is your constitutional right, the author and the publisher assume no responsibility for your actions.

Any people depicted in stock imagery provided by Thinkstock are models, and such images are being used for illustrative purposes only.
Certain stock imagery © Thinkstock.

Cover Design: Marius Spînu
www.7donkeys.eu

Cover copyright: Editura For You
www.editura-foryou.ro

Book Design: Demetra T. Tsakiroglou
www.demetrateresa.com

Print information available on the last page.

ISBN: 978-1-5043-3945-2 (sc)
ISBN: 978-1-5043-3946-9 (e)

Balboa Press rev. date: 09/16/2015

Table of Contents

Under the tree of life

I am sitting
Under the tree of life
Alone with the One
The One is the tree
The One is me
The One is you.

Daniel Mitel

PREFACE

Masters experience and teach. We learn and experience. There is a big difference. We are followers, not innovators. A Master is a conscious creator. We are trying to be conscious receivers. Trying in a world of polarity is not easy. The simple act of trying is what keeps us in an exhausting, never ending wheel of reincarnations here in this dimension.

Heart Imagery: A Path to Enlightenment provides a key to getting rid of this endless trying. Heart Imagery helps you to, once again, have a childlike consciousness, and become a re-born human being. It is a new life and an opportunity to lead your own energy to the cosmic consciousness. Why would we do this? Because we are fed up with being machines, robots; people without personalities.

We are saturated and exhausted by our own repetitive gestures, thoughts and actions. What we see today around us is a clear demonstration that the mind has failed.

When the mind fails there is just one option left: the heart.

Heart Imagery: A Path to Enlightenment is a continuation of the book **This Now Is Eternity** revealing exercises and meditations related to the most ancient spiritual system: Heart Imagery. It is a treasure full of advice, meditations and exercises coming directly from two of the last Great Masters in Heart Imagery.

These Masters lived in the Tibetan area, but that was irrelevant. Like other Great Masters of Imagery (Anastasia from Russia, Collette Aboulker-Muscat from Jerusalem or Ana Pricop from Romania), the location and the time when they lived on this planet was of no consequence. They were able to change anything: the past, the present or the future. They could reverse any action or thought. This is beyond our understanding.

Remember that everything around you is a dream and you can awaken at any moment if you really wish to.

Daniel Mitel.

ACKNOWLEDGMENT

I am grateful for your generous help and assistance; without you, this book wouldn't exist.

Thank you, Demetra Teresa Tsakiroglou, Luke Sellars, Stephen Moroz, Zlatko Kanda, Laura Iakovides, Sanela Begovic, Heather Wicks, Monica Visan, Marius Spinu and all the beloved friends that generously helped me publish this book. I ask for forgiveness if I do not remember all the names, but you are all in my heart.

Thank you from all my heart,
Daniel.

PART ONE
Learning and Experiencing

"If you understand yourself, you are free"

The Romanian Mystic and Imagery Master, Ana Pricop

CHAPTER 1

Escape the Prison of the Mind

"Masters," I said one day to my Masters, Karma Dorje and Tenzin Dhargey, "why is Heart Imagery so powerful? How is it possible to have such a strong effect from just a simple image that you give me? Is it the effect of the image or the power of my mind? I feel strong waves of energy both inside and outside me when I see or sense these images."

Karma Dorje and Tenzin Dhargey exchanged a quick look and fell silent for a moment.

There would be moments in our discussions when I could feel that something important was about to be said. This was one of them.

"Dear Tenzin, Heart Imagery helps you move into the heart and remain there. It gives you harmony and peace. You might feel one day that the whole world is collapsing and you are losing your mind. In that moment, do not be afraid that you are going insane; that is not going to happen! That moment provides the best opportunity to go into your heart," advised Tenzin Dhargey.

"What better opportunity can you have to escape the prison of the mind other than the moment when your mind stops working? All your belief patterns and preconceived ideas disappear. Your spirit is free, your consciousness is liberated and there lies the unique opportunity to slip into the heart," Karma Dorje said.

Tenzin Dhargey continued, "This is a new vision of life, dear Tenzin. You are beginning to drop your ego because you are seeing everything around you from your heart. Heart Imagery is an experience and in this experience we are all equal. We are humble co-creators. We are resurrected and we are living just in this moment. We are eternally young. Each image prepares you for the final surrender; you will see so many images on a background made by nothingness, by the eternal Universe, that suddenly you will experience your own dissolution into nothingness. You will connect with all life everywhere and you will see, sense and feel the whole Universe within you."

"Is it possible for someone who has not done any Heart Imagery exercises or any meditation techniques to experience the infinite nothingness?" I asked.

"Yes, it is possible, Karma Dorje replied and continued to explain. "We explained to you some time ago that there are eight cycles of dreaming each night. Between each cycle we literally experience a short, very short, time of pure vastness; infinite nothingness. In fact, the time that you experience the nothingness is similar to the time when you die. It is as if dying each night eight times!"

"Is it possible to go from one dream to another without passing through the nothingness?" I asked.

"Yes, it is possible," said Tenzin Darghey, "but it rarely happens. Remember what we were discussing about dreaming? There are just three possibilities. First, your dreams are a product of your subconscious mind. This situation happens almost all the time to everyone. In your dreams, it is like you are just an eye, and you see, sense and feel from the eye's perspective. You are rarely able to see your body when you dream in this way. You are just an eye. In the second case you use your dreaming body; an unconscious, but real movement of your dreaming body. You use your dreaming body in an unconscious way. Usually you realize it and get scared. When that happens, you try to wake up quickly. You try to get back into your physical body. The third situation is when a conscious and real movement of your dreaming body occurs. Not many people are able to do this. This is a very high level of consciousness."

"How can I get into my dreaming body in a conscious way?" I asked very curiously.

"First you have to understand that the dreaming body is not the physical body," said Karma Dorje. "The dreaming body is inorganic, while the physical body is organic. The dreaming body is energy in a similar form as your physical body, but just that: energy, light in a form. You will never eat in your dreaming body and if you try to, you will not be able to taste anything. This is the advantage of the physical body. On the other hand, there is no gravity or material form that can stop you when you are in the dreaming body. You can easily fly or pass through walls. You will go into your dreaming body when you are ready to use your dreaming body in a conscious way!

"The dreaming body is a level of consciousness. The more you meditate and are aware of yourself the easier the connection with the dreaming body becomes. It becomes second nature."

"Is it good to dream?" I continued asking.

Tenzin Dhargey began to describe the idea of dreaming in more detail. "Dreaming is a consequence of your desires and longings. It is what you project on the screen of your mind; it can be related to love, power, money, prestige and so on. The Masters do not dream. Dreaming corrupts vision. If you stop to analyze your dreams, you will always find something related to your ego. The ego and dreams are closely related. Once the dream is gone, the ego disappears. Remember what we told you some time ago: we are living in a dream and we are asleep even when we are awake.

"Remember the importance of the exercise '*This Is Just a Dream*' (see This Now Is Eternity in Chapter 9: '*Dreaming*'). Remember to contemplate everything around you as if it is all a dream. The houses, the people on the street, the buses, etc., all are dreams. You will have a sudden flash and feel that you are a dream too. Obviously, if the objects around you and the people around you are a dream, then you are a dream too. You are not real. When you understand that you are not real, then your ego disappears because the ego exists only in relationship to you in the dream! In that moment your dreams disappear because the dreams are just part of the decor, an interior design made by the dreaming mind. Once the dreams are gone, you will wake up totally changed. Paradoxically, you will sleep very, very deeply, but you will be awake! It is another level of consciousness! Awareness and dreaming cannot exist together, dear Tenzin," said Karma Dorje with a smile.

"Masters, why don't people meditate? Isn't meditation good? From where does this 'spiritual laziness' come from? Just thinking about the possibilities of using the dreaming body should make anybody start doing it, isn't it so?" I asked almost desperately.

I probably looked very funny because both Masters laughed until their eyes watered.

"Tenzin, Tenzin! My dear Tenzin!" Karma Dorje barely managed to say laughing. "You really want to save the world, don't you?" But, suddenly, both mystics became serious. I knew that they were going to tell me something important. Their eyes, like stars in the beautiful night sky, scrutinized me thoroughly.

"Meditation is not difficult to do if you are ready to change the direction of your focus each day," Tenzin Dhargey clarified. "Normally, you concentrate outwards. In meditation, you change the direction inwards. You literally must go within. And that usually happens when you are fed up with going outwards, running without any purpose, in all the misery of life's problems and anguish. Meditation is an art of transformation. You transform yourself through an internal journey."

"Why is it that we do not have such explanations out there?" I asked the Masters.

"Of course you do, dear Tenzin," said Tenzin Dhargey. "Think of Christianity, for instance. How many times did Jesus explain this and no one listened? Hasn't he said, 'Seek and ye shall find'? Jesus wasn't referring to Tibet, Mecca or any other place. Jesus was referring to the internal journey. Hasn't he said, 'Knock and the door shall be opened unto you'? Knock where? Outside, on the door of a house? No, of course not. Jesus was referring to the door of your Heart, the inner door. Hasn't he said, 'Ask and it shall be given'? Ask whom? Friends, the neighbors, the sky? What Jesus meant by that is to ask your inner self. Actually, Jesus said, 'Stop wasting your time and move within'. If you do, your consciousness changes completely. It is a different quality of consciousness!"

"So people must make an effort to go within, right?" I asked.

"Absolutely not!" said Karma Dorje and proceeded to explain. "Any effort to go within keeps you out! A journey remains a journey; all journeys are outward journeys. Do you understand, dear Tenzin? You are already there. You just need to stop running. When you completely stop your energy from whatever you are doing, when there is no movement at all, when there is no desire to get somewhere, when 'going' stops, then you are turned inwards. Turning inwards is not moving in, because you are already in."

"What is the best exercise to escape from the prison of mind?" I asked the Masters.

"The best way to avoid the control of the mind," said Karma Dorje, "is to breathe consciously. You can do it either as a meditation or as an exercise while shopping, walking, watching TV, and so on.

"This exercise can be done easily by anyone. Usually after ten or fifteen minutes you will feel a sort of release and a freedom that surrounds you and gives you peace and happiness.

"The exercise is very simple. First you need to move into your heart."

Moving into the Heart Exercise:

- ❖ *Close your eyes.*
- ❖ *Breathe three times (draw in a normal breath and let out a long, slow exhalation through the mouth. As you do this, see all your problems, issues, concerns and internal conflicts going out and away); then breathe in and out normally.*
- ❖ *Imagine a spiral staircase going down from the middle of your brain to the middle of your chest.*
- ❖ *Go down the stairs.*
- ❖ *Step off the stairs and slowly turn to your left.*
- ❖ *There is a door there that goes into your heart (it can be any type of door you can imagine).*
- ❖ *Open the door and step inside your heart; remember to close the door behind you.*
- ❖ *For a moment see, sense and feel the power and love emanating from your heart.*
- ❖ *Then move your attention to your breathing.*

Let's summarize:

Breathing Consciously Meditation:

- ❖ *Move to the heart.*
- ❖ *Gently move your attention to your breathing without interfering with its flow.*
- ❖ *Breathe in and out naturally and try to observe the natural and ordinary process that is taking place within you.*
- ❖ *Whenever you hear a sound around you or feel a sensation in your body, gently move your attention back to the breathing process.*
- ❖ *Continue doing this meditation as long as time allows; it can take twenty minutes or two hours.*

"This exercise," explained Tenzin Dhargey, "is completely different in the sense that you do not need to be in the silence of your meditation corner; you can do it outside, in the middle of the city and during your daily routines. Any time you remember during the day, just start breathing in a conscious way. Inhale and exhale naturally, but try to be an observer of this process. Basically your attention will split in two directions: towards your activity and to the breathing process. By doing this exercise you become very aware of your activity, very sharp and focused. The results of your activities are much better than when you do them without watching the breathing process."

CHAPTER 2

The Purpose of Life

"Masters, what is going on out there? When did humanity become so miserable? What transformations have taken place within us and have brought us to this stage of our existence?" I asked my Masters, Karma Dorje and Tenzin Dhargey.

"Tenzin," said Karma Dorje, "you must first understand that we are all born healthy and happy. Happiness has become such a rare thing because of a small group that wants you to be unhappy. However, regardless of what others want, it is you who makes the decision to be in misery or happiness. Why do you remember a Master? You remember Jesus and Buddha because they were exceptions from your daily misery. The world should be a world filled with Buddhas, with happy people that do not regard happiness as an exception to the rule. If the whole world was filled with Buddhas, believe me, you wouldn't care much about them. They would be normality."

Tenzin Dhargey continued, "There should be a natural order in your lives, dear Tenzin. If there is disorder, then you need order, isn't that so?

Therefore, the first thing that a Master does is to live in a natural way. In this way, nothing is missing. The Master becomes existence itself."

"So, do you mean that we should just live in the middle of nature? Without TVs, phones, or any other modern things that are in our lives?" I asked curiously.

"My dear Tenzin," said Karma Dorje, "there is no doubt that you can use these modern things in your daily lives. The question is, are you able to use them as simple tools, or have they turned into an addiction, a habit, a dependence. Another question has to do with the effect these things have in your lives. Has anybody had the curiosity, for example, to look into the effect that watching too much TV has on the emotional bodies? Has anybody had the desire to find out the effect of a phone on your pineal gland? Humanity has forgotten to live a life listening to classical music, reading poetry or looking at a beautiful sun. It is a luxury now to get out of the house and watch the Milky Way streaming through the night sky."

"Spirituality," said Tenzin Dhargey "comes from enjoyment, dear Tenzin. You can eat an apple with such joy and gratitude that it becomes meditation. There is a big misconception that one needs to suffer in order to become spiritual, that one needs to be a martyr in order to gain spiritual qualities. That is not true at all. If you do not enjoy this life, then how will you be able to enjoy the afterlife? If you are not able to enjoy a tree here, the green grass, the flowers, how will you ever be able to enjoy them in paradise?" he asked with a smile.

"So...," I said with a big smile, "the idea is to enjoy the moment; to live now."

"That is true, dear Tenzin. If you cannot enjoy this moment, I doubt that you will be able to enjoy the eternal. That is the whole purpose of our lives here in this dimension: to learn to enjoy the moment! There is so much philosophy regarding the purpose of life here, but remember what we are telling you now: the only reason we are here, is to enjoy the moment! And this, in fact, is the inner transformation that brings us to God's realization," Karma Dorje revealed with a smile.

"What would be the best way to enjoy life here?" I asked the Masters.

"The secret", said Tenzin Dhargey, "is to slow down. Walk slowly, eat slowly and speak slowly; move slowly. You know this already -- I see you are very good at practicing Tai Chi. I assume you feel really good when you do Tai Chi, and the reason is because you move slowly, you breathe slowly, your thoughts are gone. The result is that you become very silent within, isn't that so?"

"Yes, it is…," I almost whispered back.

"One of the things I noticed while I was in America and Europe," he continued, "was that people hurry for no reason at all. The speed of life is unbelievable. Even if there is nowhere to go, they still hurry. They are not able to see the beauty of life. All this speed makes people tense, stressed. So the first thing is to slow down. Slow down simple things, ordinary processes, and you will get peace. Why do you eat so quickly? Why would one hurry to finish their food? Your stomach does not have teeth. It is not healthy. The food remains undigested in your intestines and stays there for years; you carry pure toxins just because you hurry up when you eat. Eat slowly; chew your food until it becomes liquid. In fact, you must know that one needs to chew their food 27 times, 54 times or 108 times. A minimum of 27 times!

"When you have nothing to do, do not try to find something. Just sit silently and look at the grass. Just sit silently and look at the stars. Just sit silently and close your eyes. Breathe in and breathe out completely relaxed. You might even stop breathing from time to time. Do not panic. Let it be. Enjoy the moment. How nice it is to float in the universe doing nothing, just connecting with yourself. When you find this peace, then you know what life is."

"What is the best exercise to help us understand the purpose of life?" I asked the Masters.

"Dear Tenzin", said Karma Dorje with a smile, "this is a tricky question in the sense that all of these exercises and activities make us understand the purpose of life."

"However," he continued, "the best process to understand the purpose of life is the contemplation process. Daily contemplation of Mother Nature brings us closer and closer to understanding the Universe and life itself.

"The Contemplation Exercise is very easy. Find a place in the middle of nature where you feel comfortable and relaxed. It can be in a garden or in a park, a place surrounded by the trees, grass, flowers, animals and birds. This exercise is very easy:

Contemplation Exercise:

- ❖ *Move into the Heart (see <u>Moving into the Heart</u>).*
- ❖ *If your eyes are closed, open them and start to contemplate the nature around you.*
- ❖ *You can either let your eyes see more elements of Mother Earth or, after a minute or so, you can choose a specific part of nature, a tree, a flower, the grass, etc., and look at it.*
- ❖ *Become completely detached and let your eyes rest on Mother Nature without analyzing the surroundings around you.*
- ❖ *Continue doing this until you feel connected with Mother Nature, part of Mother Nature's process and activities.*

"Soon you will feel a sense of completion, realization and fulfillment. You will start to understand the language of nature around you; you will see, sense and feel in a different way. Your life will integrate with the perfection of the Universe, of Divinity.

"Furthermore," Tenzin Dhargey said, "you will see, sense and feel your role in this beautiful place"

CHAPTER 3

We Need Clarity

Masters, why do we see things so wrongly? What is triggered in our mind that makes us choose our paths so abnormally, in such a difficult way? Is it our combination of thoughts?" I asked Karma Dorje and Tenzin Dhargey.

"First," said Tenzin Dhargey, "try to understand that our thoughts are energy; and even more importantly, our thoughts have individuality. Our thoughts move very fast, like any other energy. They move so quickly, that we are not able to see or sense the interval that exists between two thoughts. But make no mistake: the interval is there! The fact that we cannot perceive it does not mean that it does not exist. In fact, that interval is the real you! Your mind is not you. Your thoughts are not you. If you take all your thoughts away, what will remain of your mind? Nothing. The mind itself does not exist. The only thing that exists is thinking. Because you do not stop thinking, you cannot see your path clearly. How can you see it when you have so many thoughts that jeopardize your view?"

"We need coherence, we need lucidity and we need clarity," I whispered to myself.

"That is true, dear Tenzin," said Karma Dorje. "You need clarity. You need to be alert between your thoughts. You need to look into that interval, into that space that exists between your thoughts. You need to work your no-mind state of being. Once your mind pops in, you lose the real you. You are clouded, confused; there is no clarity anymore."

"But, if I am thinking about achieving "no mind", that is also a thought," I observed. "If I am thinking that I am enlightened, this is another thought. All those who trumpet that they are masters and great teachers are, in fact, putting a thought out there. They are displaying their mind, their ego."

"True," said Tenzin Dhargey. "But they are actually trying. They are trying to be loving, peaceful, in harmony. However, whenever they try, it is just a try-out, it is a thought. Once you get in that no-mind interval and see clearly, you do not need to display anything. Your quietness and silence is veritable and authentic. You are transparent like a mountain lake. You have clarity.

"There is a simple and powerful meditation that brings you to clarity."

Clarity meditation:

- ❖ *Move into the Heart (see <u>Moving into the Heart</u>).*
- ❖ *Look around you and see the universe of the heart; you might see something there or you might just feel the energy of the heart.*
- ❖ *Whatever it is that you see or feel, let it happen; do not interfere with your thoughts or will power; just stay there and do nothing.*
- ❖ *Now, find a comfortable place to sit; you may want to sit on a chair or in a half lotus posture.*
- ❖ *Think about all of the thoughts or actions that keep you in confusion; anything that creates confusion within you; it can be related to your*

spiritual path or your material path; it can be spiritual confusion or material confusion.

❖ *Now STOP thinking or seeing anything; stay in total silence in your heart for a few minutes and do nothing; just remain there in silence.*

❖ *Suddenly, in this silence you will clearly see a response to your confused thoughts or actions; you will know what to do; you will have an answer to your dilemma.*

❖ *The answer might come as a sudden thought in the middle of the silence, or you might feel like you are walking in the middle of a forest, lost, and suddenly you see the path. You might see somebody giving you a message or a gift.*

❖ *Continue sitting there, in your heart, in silence and quietness until you feel ready to come back. Then open your eyes.*

"This meditation," explained Karma Dorje, "is very important when you need to see clearly, to quieten your mind and make a decision. You need to stop doing everything else; otherwise anything you do will be based on confusion, on doubt and ignorance. If you are confused and lost, how do you expect to make a clear decision? If you do not stop what you were doing then all your actions will be based on confusion, lack of clarity and uncertainty. If you are lost and confused in the middle of an unknown city, what are you going to do? Are you going to run around continuously trying to find the place you are looking for? No, of course not! You need to stop running, rest for a few minutes, let all your thoughts go away and, suddenly, you will have clarity."

"Is this a way of feeling and 'seeing with the third eye?" I asked the Masters.

"It certainly helps to see, sense and feel using your third eye," he replied. "There is another exercise to feel your third eye. It is easy to do and the results are outstanding.

Feel your third eye exercise:

- ❖ *Move into the Heart (see <u>Moving into the Heart</u>).*
- ❖ *Close your eyes and gently cross them; imagine that there is a line connecting the point between your eyebrows with the middle of your forehead; start looking at the point between your eyebrows and go up slowly-slowly until you arrive to the middle of your forehead.*
- ❖ *Repeat this eyes movement couple of times and suddenly your eyes will stop in a very comfortable position; feel the point and suddenly your eyes will become fixed; if it is difficult to move them, then you know that you have found the right point.*
- ❖ *Keep your attention on this point and you will suddenly experience an interesting phenomenon: you will witness your thoughts running in front of you as if you are watching them on a film screen; you will see your thoughts passing by like clouds in the blue sky.*
- ❖ *Now move your attention to breathing; try to keep your eyes on the point; you will be able to feel your subtle and delicate vibration of breathing; you can observe now the essence of prana.*

CHAPTER 4

The Seven Ancient Heart Imagery Exercises

A re there any physical exercises or specific breathing techniques involved in the Heart Imagery system?" I asked the Masters.

"Yes," replied Karma Dorje. "There are a set of seven exercises that were brought here some years ago from a Tibetan monastery by an Englishman. He had spent time with a group of Masters, similarly to how you are doing today here with us."

"We have noticed," continued Tenzin Dhargey, "that only five of the exercises are used in the spiritual communities outside of Tibet, and they are not used correctly. The breathing technique had never been explained properly: how each breath is supposed to be coordinated with physical movement".

"The most important part of the exercises, which is the breathing, must be understood correctly if we wish to have any effect energetically out of it," continued Karma Dorje.

"All seven exercises are to be performed using Reversed Breathing; reversed breathing is the same way as normal breathing, just as you do in your morning Tai Chi, dear Tenzin."

Indeed when I do Tai Chi, I breathe opposite to Natural Breathing. In Natural Breathing, as we inhale, we expand our stomach and abdomen, in contraction, and we bring it back as we exhale. Natural breathing is also called "Post-Birth Breathing" as it is the normal breathing system we use after our birth.

However, Reversed Breathing is completely opposite to Natural Breathing. This means that, when we inhale, we contract the stomach and abdomen and, when we exhale, we relax it and expand. At the same time, when we inhale, we gently contract our perineum muscle at the base of our body. When we contract our perineum muscle at the base of our body, there is also a slight contraction of our genitals and anus muscle.

Reversed breathing is widely used in some traditional spiritual schools: Tai Chi, Qi Gong, Kriya Yoga, Kundalini Yoga and some other spiritual systems.

"People believe that these exercises are Tibetan, but it is not true. These exercises come from the same source as Heart Imagery: the Adamic Race. In fact, these exercises are considered to be the 'physical' component of Heart Imagery," Karma Dorje said.

"The effect of doing these seven exercises is beyond that which the human mind can understand, dear Tenzin," continued Karma Dorje with a smile.

Tenzin Dhargey described the effect of the exercises. "Many practitioners experience a sense of gaining strength, becoming more powerful, even younger. However, when we talk about Heart Imagery, the most important result for us is the cleaning of the mind and connecting our energy to Source, to the Pranic Ocean of the Universe that is around and within us."

"Some people," continued Tenzin Dhargey, "believe that one needs a strong body to do these exercises, especially exercises number two, four and five, but it is not about body. It is about a strong desire and will to do them. Of course, if your physical body has a problem you can choose to do just some exercises that are suitable for your condition."

"It is imperative that these exercises are done on an empty stomach and before beginning the Heart Imagery exercises," Karma Dorje pointed out. "They are usually done in sets of three. So, if you do three of each, you perform a total of twenty-one exercises. You can go up to six, nine, twelve, fifteen or twenty-one of each. If you do twenty-one of each exercise, you reach one hundred forty-seven exercises, which require much time and a great desire to do it! Between each exercise, it is good to pause for five to ten-seconds."

"When you perform the exercises," continued Tenzin Dhargey, "you must use a specific mantra that charges your cells: 'I am pure love and bliss, I am in light and peace'. This mantra must be done on each inhale and exhale. When you breathe in, you usually mentally chant the first half of the mantra: 'I am pure love and bliss' and when you breathe out you chant the second part: 'I am in light and peace'."

"Other than cleaning the mind and preparing for Heart Imagery, do these exercises have any other effect?" I asked the Masters.

"Yes, they do have another powerful effect, dear Tenzin. These exercises help you release and dissolve chronic tensions and emotional traumas that have stacked been up in your body for years; maybe for lives," explained Karma Dorje.

"There are three places in our bodies where the emotional traumas are stored," continued Tenzin Dhargey. "They are the psoas muscles, the heart muscle and the central and lower part of our brain. If we have a traumatic experience, three things are happen. First, the psoas muscles, which are located on the side lumbar region of the spine protecting the edge of the pelvis, start to contract and remain contracted until the danger or the shock is over. Secondly, the heart muscle goes into a similar deep chronic tension, until the emotional trauma is gone. Thirdly, inside our brain, both the pituitary and pineal gland, store the traumatic experience until it is over."

As he prepared to show me the exercises, Karma Dorje said, "The Seven Ancient Heart Imagery Exercises are designed to release tension from these three locations. The effect these exercises have is that they reverberate throughout these three powerful centers and naturally dissolve any emotional trauma."

The Seven Ancient Heart Imagery Exercises - Exercise One ("the Wheel")

❖ *Place the tip of your tongue on the roof of your mouth; roll your tongue backwards as much as possible; if you can touch the uvula or even go deeper inside the nasal cavity, then you can literally help your energy move up into the brain and work with your pituitary and pineal gland.*

❖ *Stand up keeping your arms outstretched with both palms facing the ground; the distance between your feet must be the same as the distance between your shoulders.*

❖ *Spin around from left to right (clockwise as if you would see it from above) a couple of times; keep your eyes opened and when you get slightly dizzy, stop.*

❖ *Facing the east and with both palms united at the level of your chest (as if you are praying), inhale using the reversed breathing and mentally chant the mantra "I am pure love and bliss".*

❖ *Exhale and slightly open your palms as if you are pushing an invisible wall in front of you and mentally chant the mantra: "I am in light and peace".*

❖ *Do at least 12 sets of inhalations and exhalations after each spin.*

❖ *Do three, six, nine or twelve spins.*

❖ *Keeping your eyes opened you will also be able to experience the rotation of your Mer-Ka-Ba (Body of Light)*

❖ *When you finish the whole exercise do it one more time mentally with your eyes closed; try to feel the effect of the exercise even if you are not doing it physically.*

The Seven Ancient Heart Imagery Exercises - Exercise Two ("Tibetan Abs")

❖ *Place the tip of your tongue on the roof of your mouth; roll your tongue backwards as much as possible; if you can touch the uvula or even go deeper inside the nasal cavity, then you can literally help your energy move up into the brain and work with your pituitary and pineal gland.*

❖ *Lie full length on a yoga mat with hands down near the hips.*

❖ *Inhale using the reversed breathing and raise the legs straight up without bending the knees; at the same time, raise your head.*

❖ *You might find it helpful to gently contract your hands when you bring your legs and head up and relax them when you exhale and lower your head and feet.*

❖ *Hold this position for three-seconds and exhale lowering the feet to the floor and the head at the same time.*

❖ *Do three, six, nine or twelve sets.*

❖ *When you finish the whole exercise do it one more time mentally with your eyes closed; try to feel the effect of the exercise even if you are not doing it physically.*

The Seven Ancient Heart Imagery Exercises - Exercise Three ("the Wall")

❖ *Place the tip of your tongue on the roof of your mouth; roll your tongue backwards as much as possible; if you can touch the uvula or even go deeper inside the nasal cavity, then you can literally help your energy move up into the brain and work with your pituitary and pineal gland.*

❖ *Kneel on a yoga mat with your hands at your sides and your palms flat against the side of your legs.*

❖ *Inhale using the reversed breathing and lower your chin on your chest.*

❖ *Hold your breath for three-seconds and then exhale placing your fists on the kidneys and with both thumbs pressing gently on the third chakra (the point on the spine right behind your navel).*

❖ *Bend the head backwards as far as possible, while also bending your waist; your toes will prevent you from falling over backwards.*

❖ *Hold your breath for three-seconds (you are empty) and do another set.*

❖ *Do three, six, nine or twelve sets.*

❖ *When you finish the whole exercise do it one more time mentally with your eyes closed; try to feel the effect of the exercise even if you are not doing it physically.*

The Seven Ancient Heart Imagery Exercises - Exercise Four ("the Table")

❖ *Place the tip of your tongue on the roof of your mouth; roll your tongue backwards as much as possible; if you can touch the uvula or even go deeper inside the nasal cavity, then you can literally help your energy move up into the brain and work with your pituitary and pineal gland.*

❖ *Sit on a yoga mat keeping your spine as straight as possible and your palms flat on the rug; the legs must be perfectly straight*

❖ *Lower your chin until it almost touches your chest; then inhale using the reversed breathing. As you inhale, raise your body, and at the same time, bend your knees so that your legs, from the knees down, are practically straight up and down.*

❖ *Hold this position for three seconds, and exhale returning to the initial position.*

❖ *Hold your breath for three-seconds (you are empty) and do another set.*

❖ *Do three, six, nine or twelve sets.*

❖ *When you finish the whole exercise do it one more time mentally with your eyes closed; try to feel the effect of the exercise even if you are not doing it physically.*

The Seven Ancient Heart Imagery Exercises - Exercise Five ("the Dog and the Snake")

❖ *Place the tip of your tongue on the roof of your mouth; roll your tongue backwards as much as possible; if you can touch the uvula or even go deeper inside the nasal cavity, then you can literally help your energy move up into the brain and work with your pituitary and pineal gland.*

❖ *Place your hands on the floor about a shoulder distance apart.*

❖ *Inhale using the reversed breathing while keeping the legs stretched out towards the rear with your feet also about a shoulder distance apart. Push your body up as far as possible, rising on the toes and hands; the chin lowers until it touches the chest.*

❖ *Hold your breath for three-seconds.*

❖ *Exhale and relax your navel and perineum muscles and allow your body to slowly come down to the yoga system's 'snake posture - cobra position'.*

❖ *Hold your breath for three-seconds (you are empty) and do another set.*

❖ *Do three, six, nine or twelve sets.*

❖ *When you finish the whole exercise do it one more time mentally with your eyes closed; try to feel the effect of the exercise even if you are not doing it physically.*

The Seven Ancient Heart Imagery Exercises - Exercise Six ("the Emptiness")

❖ *Place the tip of your tongue on the roof of your mouth; roll your tongue backwards as much as possible; if you can touch the uvula or even go deeper inside the nasal cavity, then you can literally help your energy move up into the brain and work with your pituitary and pineal gland.*

❖ *Normal posture: either stand up and stand straight breathing out completely or sit down on a chair or on a pillow on a yoga mat in the half-lotus posture.*

❖ *Bend over forward putting your hands on your knees, forcing out the last trace of air.*

❖ *With empty lungs, return to the standing straight posture.*

❖ *Place your hands on your waist and push your shoulders up by pressing down with your hands. Pull the abdomen in as much as possible and raise your chest, keeping your lungs empty.*

❖ *Hold this position as long as you are able to on empty lungs.*

❖ *Breathe in through the nose until your lungs are full.*

❖ *Exhale through the mouth, allowing your arms to relax and hang free.*

❖ *Take several deep breaths before the next repetition.*

❖ *Do three, four or maximum five sets.*

❖ *When you finish the whole exercise do it one more time mentally with your eyes closed; try to feel the effect of the exercise even if you are not doing it physically.*

The Seven Ancient Heart Imagery Exercises - Exercise Seven ("the Sphere")

In exercise seven we utilize some movements of the head.

❖ *Again, place the tip of your tongue on the roof of your mouth; roll your tongue backwards as much as possible; if you can touch the uvula or even go deeper inside the nasal cavity, then you can literally help your energy move up into the brain and work with your pituitary and pineal gland.*

❖ *Inhale (reversed breathing) and, as you hold your breath, bend your head forwards. Feel the energy that is present in the frontal region of your head. Without raising your chin to its normal position, slowly guide your head to the position in which the head is bent towards the left shoulder – as if you are trying to touch your left shoulder with your left ear. Feel the energy that is present in the left side of the brain (over your left ear).*

❖ *From this position, slowly guide both your head and the flow of energy backwards to the occipital region of the brain.*

❖ *Slowly guide your head to the position in which the head is bent towards your right shoulder – are trying to touch your right shoulder with the right ear.*

❖ *As always, feel the flow of energy moving to each position.*

❖ *Slowly return to the initial position with the head bent forwards. Now, slowly straighten your head and return with your chin parallel to the ground, while you gently exhale.*

❖ *For 10 seconds your attention will move towards the central part of your brain (the Cave of Brahma) under the fontanelle.*

❖ *Do three, six, nine or twelve sets.*

The Seven Ancient Heart Imagery Exercises - Exercise One ("The Wheel")

The Seven Ancient Heart Imagery Exercises - Exercise Two ("Tibetan Abs")

The Seven Ancient Heart Imagery Exercises - Exercise Three ("The Wall")

The Seven Ancient Heart Imagery Exercises - Exercise Four ("The Table")

The Seven Ancient Heart Imagery Exercises - Exercise Five ("The Dog and The Snake")

The Seven Ancient Heart Imagery Exercises - Exercise Six ("The Emptiness")

The Seven Ancient Heart Imagery Exercises - Exercise Seven ("The Sphere")

PART TWO

Heart Imagery with Pictures, Sacred Geometry and Holy Teachings

*"With God, two I's cannot find room. You say 'I' and He says 'I'.
Either you die before Him, or let Him die before you; then duality
will not remain. But it is impossible for Him to die, either subjectively
or objectively, since He is the Living God, the Undying."*

The Spiritual Teachings of Rumi XXV 58

CHAPTER 5

Heart Imagery with Pictures and Sacred Geometry

S o in a way, we are deceiving ourselves; everything around us is just our own dreams, our own projections. We are the only ones responsible, isn't that so?" I asked the Masters.

"That is perfectly true, dear Tenzin," said Karma Dorje. "Try for one day to see everything around you without allowing your mind to say anything. Look at a picture or a painting without letting your mind judge it. Do not say 'lovely' or 'terrible!' Be neutral, completely detached. The more you put your mind aside, the more you let the light fill you and then reach the truth.

"Look at this picture!" said the Master as he showed me a simple old post card with a splendid photo of the Grand Canyon.

"Close your eyes! Now!" he demanded, before I could even wonder where he got the card from.

"Now go into your heart," he continued. "Open your eyes again and look at the image for a moment, then close your eyes and see the image within your heart."

A warm energy and feeling began to envelope me like the sweet touch of an invisible hand. The photo was almost alive within my heart.

For a couple of minutes I felt different; detached from all of the world's thoughts and issues. I felt like I was the creator of that image.

"Nice, isn't it?" he asked smiling.

This chapter helps you achieve harmony, peace, healing and balancing of your mental, emotional and physical bodies. The technique is very simple and efficient.

Just move into your heart and open your eyes for five seconds and look at the image in front of you. Then close your eyes and see the same image in your heart.

You can stay for just a few seconds with your eyes closed feeling the effect of the image, or for a couple of minutes. You might cry, or laugh. You might even fall asleep; your mental, emotional and physical bodies will harmonize after a few images.

You can do this exercise outdoors in the middle of nature or even indoors by looking at some beautiful pictures of nature. You can also use sacred geometry pictures.

Each image, whether it is a photo or a sacred geometry picture, has a multiple effect on your chakras and bodies. The maximum effect of these pictures is achieved during the Heart Imagery workshops under the guidance of a Master of Imagery. In the workshops that I hold throughout the world, I have witnessed incredible change of energies during these exercises. I, therefore, strongly encourage you to attend a Heart Imagery workshop. You can find the schedule of workshops held world-wide at ***www.danielmitel.com.***

Before doing these exercises, you must move your spirit from your brain into your heart.

Moving into the Heart Exercise

❖ *Close your eyes.*

❖ *Breathe three times (draw in a normal breath and let out a long, slow exhalation through the mouth. As you do this, see all your problems, issues, concerns and internal conflicts going out and away); then breathe in and out normally.*

❖ *Imagine a spiral staircase going down from the middle of your brain to the middle of your chest.*

❖ *Go down the stairs.*

❖ *Step off the stairs and slowly turn to your left.*

❖ *There is a door there that goes into your heart (it can be any type of door you can imagine).*

❖ *Open the door and step inside your heart; remember to close the door behind you.*

❖ *For a moment see, sense and feel the power and love emanating from your heart.*

Practice the "Moving into the Heart" exercise a couple of times until you get used to perceiving the difference between being in the brain and being in the heart.

Let's do a simple exercise in order to see, sense and feel how this spiritual technique works. We will use three images: a beautiful picture of nature, an eagle and a sacred geometry image, hidden in which you will find the most powerful sacred geometry image used for thousands and thousands of years by all spiritual schools: the flower of life.

Do not judge or analyze what you see there. Relax in your chair and let the image "speak" to you!

SET 1

- ❖ *Move into the Heart.*
- ❖ *Open your eyes and look at the image for five seconds and then gently close your eyes. Remember the image you saw a couple of seconds ago and see it now in front of you, within your heart. See, sense and feel the energy emanating from it.*
- ❖ *Let your mental, emotional and physical bodies balance and harmonize; anything you feel within your heart, let it be.*
- ❖ *Stay for 10-15 seconds and enjoy the energy from the image then let it dissolve in the Universe, breathe and open your eyes looking at the next picture; then repeat it with the third picture.*
- ❖ *After you have done a set of three pictures relax at least 2-3 minutes until you do the next set.*

On my website there is a page dedicated to this spiritual work with 27 sets. Visit this page at: ***http://danielmitel.com/heart-imagery-book/*** and after a simple registration you will receive an email message with the password that gives you access to 27 sets of unbelievably powerful images!

CHAPTER 6

Heart Imagery with the Enlightened Ones

Are there any Heart Imagery exercises in the spiritual work of other Masters?" I asked the Masters.

"All paths of God to realization on this planet are deeply connected with Heart Imagery, dear Tenzin," said Karma Dorjec. "It does not matter whether you speak about Jesus or Buddha, about Rumi or Shiva. All of them use Heart Imagery. Moses used Heart Imagery. The Masters of Tai Chi, Qi Gong and Martial Arts use Heart Imagery. Naguals and shamans use Heart Imagery. There is even a Heart Imagery Master in the forests of Siberia in Russia that uses Heart Imagery on a daily basis. Her teachings will change the perception of a lot of people regarding the way they live."

Indeed, a few years later I found out about the invaluable teachings of Anastasia, the Siberian Master.

"But I've read Rumi's teachings and haven't found any mention of Heart Imagery there. I've also read the Bible, the Koran and the Zohar, and haven't seen it mentioned there either. I've also read 'The Prophet' by Kahlil of Gibran and haven't discovered heart imagery there," I exclaimed disappointedly.

"That's because you were not present there, my beloved Tenzin," Tenzin Dhargey said with a smile. "Who was reading these holy books? You or your mind? How did you read them? Like a mathematical exercise or when you felt the call to read them? Did you analyze each book as an equation or close your eyes and contemplate on the teachings of each book?"

"Even 'I Ching' - the Book of Changes - has a heart imagery system behind each hexagram," added Karma Dorje. "Tarot is not just a pack of playing cards. Each pictogram has an imagery sense and meaning."

I really felt embarrassed because I realized that they were right. I had been reading all these books as simple lectures, without feeling the real message behind them.

"Do not worry, dear Tenzin," said Karma Dorje seeing my discomfort. "Now you will read the very same books as if they are completely different! Do not be disappointed. It is part of your evolution and understanding."

"In order to better understand what we are telling you, we will do some exercises together," Tenzin Dhargey said.

I remember some of the exercises very well, but there are others that remain within my heart, waiting for me to find them.

Before doing these exercises, I must remind you to do the "Moving into the Heart" exercise. This is the most important exercise from this book, as it helps you to realize the vibration of your heart. Practice this exercise when you wake up; it takes 10-15 seconds to do it. Before you speak, go into your heart. Before doing anything -- eating, speaking, working, making love, reading, etc. -- go into your heart.

Moving into the Heart Exercise

❖ *Close your eyes.*

❖ *Breathe three times (draw in a normal breath and let out a long, slow exhalation through the mouth. As you do this, see all your problems, issues, concerns and internal conflicts going out and away); then breathe in and out normally.*

❖ *Imagine a spiral staircase going down from the middle of your brain to the middle of your chest.*

❖ *Go down the stairs.*

❖ *Step off the stairs and slowly turn to your left.*

❖ *There is a door there that goes into your heart (it can be any type of door you can imagine).*

❖ *Open the door and step inside your heart; remember to close the door behind you.*

❖ *For a moment see, sense and feel the power and love emanating from your heart.*

Practical Heart Imagery Exercises from Holy Books and Great Masters

The Spiritual Teachings of Rumi Imagery Exercise (1)

❖ *Move into the Heart (see <u>Moving into the Heart</u>).*

❖ *Breathe out once (exhale deeply and slowly through the mouth).*

❖ *See, sense and feel that hundreds of thousands of men are hidden within a single man.*

❖ *See, sense and feel that hundreds of thousands of women are hidden within a single woman.*

❖ *See, sense and feel that a hundred bows and arrows are contained in a single dart.*

❖ *Breathe out once and open your eyes.*

❖ *Write down your experience.*

The Spiritual Teachings of Rumi Imagery Exercise (2)

❖ *Move into the Heart (see <u>Moving into the Heart</u>).*

❖ *Breathe out once (exhale deeply and slowly through the mouth).*

❖ *See, sense and feel that Spring and Summer are an expansion and Autumn and Winter are a contraction.*

❖ *See, sense and feel the garden of your heart, green and fresh and new, full of rosebuds and cypress and jasmine.*

❖ *See, sense and feel that you are dust and that you grow into multicolored roses.*

❖ *Breathe out once and open your eyes.*

❖ *Write down your experience.*

The Spiritual Teachings of Rumi Imagery Exercise (3)

❖ *Move into the Heart (see <u>Moving into the Heart</u>).*

❖ *Breathe out once (a long, slow exhalation through your mouth).*

❖ *See, sense and feel that your body is a garden full of roses; your heart is a temple in this beautiful garden.*

❖ *See, sense and feel that if only you would open the door of this temple for an instant, you would see that the heart of every existing thing is your intimate friend.*

❖ *See, sense and feel that in the everlasting Presence, you are the Witness and the Witnessed.*

❖ *Breathe out once and open your eyes.*

❖ *Write down your experience.*

The Spiritual Teachings of Rumi Imagery Exercise (4)

❖ *Move into the Heart (see <u>Moving into the Heart</u>).*

❖ *Breathe out once (a long, slow exhalation through your mouth).*

❖ *See, sense and feel that the Heart is the antechamber of the eye: for certain, everything that reaches the heart will enter from the eye and will become a form.*

- ❖ *See, sense and feel that in order to find your True Self, you must pass beyond your illusory self.*
- ❖ *See, sense and feel that when you sacrifice your intellect for the love for God, He will give you 10 times more like it, or seven hundred times.*
- ❖ *Breathe out once and open your eyes.*
- ❖ *Write down your experience.*

The Spiritual Teachings of the Bible Imagery Exercise (5)

- ❖ *Move into the Heart (see <u>Moving into the Heart</u>).*
- ❖ *Breathe out once (a long, slow exhalation through your mouth).*
- ❖ *See, sense and feel that you can create or call Light into your heart; look around and do it like the Creator; say "Let there be light" then wait to see or feel the Light coming into your Heart.*
- ❖ *See, sense and feel every living creature enjoying their time on Noah's Ark; see, sense and feel the unlimited ocean around the Ark.*
- ❖ *Breathe out once and open your eyes.*
- ❖ *Write down your experience.*

The Spiritual Teachings of I Ching Imagery Exercise (6)

- ❖ *Move into the Heart (see <u>Moving into the Heart</u>).*
- ❖ *Breathe out once (a long, slow exhalation through your mouth).*
- ❖ *See, sense, feel and understand that I Ching, the Book of Changes or the Book of Wisdom, helps you generate a personal insight about your past, present and future.*
- ❖ *See, sense, feel and understand the eight trigrams: sky, water, mountain, thunder, wind, fire, earth and rain.*
- ❖ *See, sense and feel that:*
    the sky makes you creative and strong;
    the water makes you understand difficulties and danger;
    the mountain gives you stillness and tranquility;
    the thunder helps you expand and have initiative;

> *the wind makes you gentle and honest;*
> *the fire gives you clarity and makes you conscious;*
> *the earth makes you receptive and adaptive;*
> *the rain gives you fullness and openness;*

❖ *Breathe out once and open your eyes.*

❖ *Write down your experience.*

The Spiritual Teachings of I Ching Imagery Exercise (7)

❖ *Move into the Heart (see <u>Moving into the Heart</u>).*

❖ *Breathe out once (a long, slow exhalation through your mouth).*

❖ *See, sense and feel that the force of the cosmos is boundless and unlimited.*

❖ *See, sense and feel the Image of Beginning.*

❖ *See, sense and feel that inexperience helps you advance in your spiritual path and brings you wisdom.*

❖ *Breathe out once and open your eyes.*

❖ *Write down your experience.*

The Spiritual Teachings of I Ching Imagery Exercise (8)

❖ *Move into the Heart (see <u>Moving into the Heart</u>).*

❖ *Breathe out once (a long, slow exhalation through your mouth).*

❖ *See, sense and feel the Flow of The Universe.*

❖ *See, sense and feel that you have patience and determination; know that these two qualities bring advancement in your spiritual journey.*

❖ *See, sense and feel that truth is hidden in any conflict; remember to plan carefully before taking action and understand that winning a conflict will only result in repeated future conflicts.*

❖ *Breathe out once and open your eyes.*

❖ *Write down your experience.*

The Spiritual Teachings of I Ching Imagery Exercise (9)

❖ *Move into the Heart (see <u>Moving into the Heart</u>).*
❖ *Breathe out once (a long, slow exhalation through your mouth).*
❖ *See, sense and feel that any noble spirit brings good fortune and no mistakes are done.*
❖ *See, sense and feel that any wise leader corrects a situation with moderation.*
❖ *See, sense and feel that inferior persons crave success, but that will lead them to misfortune and problems.*
❖ *Breathe out once and open your eyes.*
❖ *Write down your experience.*

The Spiritual Teachings of I Ching Imagery Exercise (10)

❖ *Move into the Heart (see <u>Moving into the Heart</u>).*
❖ *Breathe out once (a long, slow exhalation through your mouth).*
❖ *See, sense and feel the Image of Unity.*
❖ *See, sense and feel that through sincerity and honesty with others you build strong relationships.*
❖ *See, sense and feel that you can achieve your goal by staying generous and humble in your behavior.*
❖ *Breathe out once and open your eyes.*
❖ *Write down your experience.*

The Spiritual Teachings of Kahlil Gibran Imagery Exercise (11)

❖ *Move into the Heart (see Moving into the Heart).*
❖ *Breathe out once (a long, slow exhalation through your mouth).*
❖ *See, sense and feel that when you love you should not say, "God is in my heart," but rather, "I am in the heart of God."*
❖ *See, sense and feel that you cannot direct the course of love; for love, if it finds you worthy, directs your course.*

❖ *See, sense and feel yourself saying a prayer for your beloved in your heart and a song of praise upon your lips.*

❖ *Breathe out once and open your eyes.*

❖ *Write down your experience.*

The Spiritual Teachings of Kahlil Gibran Imagery Exercise (12)

❖ *Move into the Heart (see <u>Moving into the Heart</u>).*

❖ *Breathe out once (a long, slow exhalation through your mouth).*

❖ *See, sense and feel that joy and sorrow are inseparable; the deeper that sorrow carves into your being, the more joy you can contain.*

❖ *See, sense and feel that when the storm comes and the mighty wind shakes the forest, you can say in awe, "God moves in passion."*

❖ *See, sense and feel that you are a breath in God's sphere and a leaf in God's forest.*

❖ *Breathe out once and open your eyes.*

❖ *Write down your experience.*

CHAPTER 7

Connecting with Our Ancestors
and Mother Nature

Is Heart Imagery connected with our ancestors? How can we reconnect with whom we really are and with our roots? How can we reconnect with Mother Nature using Heart Imagery exercises?" I asked my Masters, Karma Dorje and Tenzin Dhargey.

"Heart Imagery is a language we use," said Karma Dorje with a smile. ""It is the language of images, which is the most powerful connector between us and our ancestors. The inter-dimensional conversations take place with images. I remember when I visited western countries how people talked about crop circles. They were happy that other civilizations from other planets contacted us, but they were puzzled as to why they used this method of communication. But what other means of communication can there be between us other than images? This is the easiest way for them to communicate with us on this planet, isn't it?"

"Unless we are able to meet our ancestors through meditation, the only other way to communicate with them is through Heart Imagery," continued Tenzin Dhargey.

"Does the same apply to Mother Nature?" I asked the Masters.

"Correct. The best way to communicate with Mother Earth is through Heart Imagery and meditation," Tenzin Dhargey replied.

The following four Heart Imagery exercises are powerful instruments that help us reconnect with our ancestors and with Mother Nature. They can be done anytime and anywhere. The only requirement is to remain in silence and let each image speak to you.

First and foremost, remember the **Heart Meditation** steps:

- ❖ *Move into the Heart (see <u>Moving into the Heart</u>).*
- ❖ *Close your eyes.*
- ❖ *Breathe three times (draw in a normal breath and let out a long, slow exhalation through the mouth. As you do this, see all your problems, issues, concerns and internal conflicts going out and away); then breathe in and out normally.*
- ❖ *Imagine a spiral staircase going down from the middle of your brain to the middle of your chest.*
- ❖ *Go down the stairs.*
- ❖ *Step off the stairs and slowly turn to your left.*
- ❖ *There is a door there that goes into your heart (it can be any type of door you can imagine).*
- ❖ *Open the door and step inside your heart; remember to close the door behind you.*
- ❖ *For a moment see, sense and feel the power and love emanating from your heart.*

The Sacred Place Exercise (1)

- ❖ *Move into the Heart (see <u>Moving into the Heart</u>).*
- ❖ *Breathe out once (a long, slow exhalation through your mouth).*
- ❖ *See, sense and feel that the Heart is the sacred meeting place where you and your Ancestors are about to communicate.*

❖ *See, sense and feel that you need to prepare this holy place: let the Inner Light come in, allow the Inner Sound to resonate and let the Pure Energy manifest; let the divine colors reveal themselves within your Heart.*

❖ *Now let yourself enjoy the sacred meeting place where you will meet your Ancestors: find a comfortable place there and contemplate the surroundings.*

❖ *Breathe out once and open your eyes.*

❖ *Write down your experience.*

The Spiritual Teaching of the Ancestors Exercise (2)

❖ *Move into the Heart (see <u>Moving into the Heart</u>).*

❖ *Breathe out once (a long, slow exhalation through your mouth).*

❖ *See, sense, feel and know that you are ready to meet your Ancestors.*

❖ *Know that Your Higher Self is the helper and the assistant between you and the Ancestors.*

❖ *See the Universe in front of you; start moving between stars, planets and galaxies until you find the Sphere of The Ancestors.*

❖ *See, sense, feel and know that your Ancestors are ready to communicate with you; listen to what they have to tell you.*

❖ *The Ancestors are guiding you to Mother Earth; She appears in front of you; listen to what She has to say to you.*

❖ *Now The Ancestors are guiding you to Father Sun; He appears in front of you; listen to what He has to say to you.*

❖ *See and feel that you are part of the Universe; you are the Cosmic Child of Mother Earth and Father Sun.*

❖ *Breathe out once and open your eyes.*

❖ *Write down your experience.*

The Contemplation Place Exercise (3)

❖ *Move into the Heart (see <u>Moving into the Heart</u>).*

❖ *Breathe out once (let out a long, slow exhalation through your mouth).*

- ❖ *See, sense and feel that you are in the middle of the heart and from there you can see trees and forests.*
- ❖ *Watch how the trees are speaking to you; their movements are showing the Cosmic letters;*
- ❖ *Feel how you can breathe with them; inhale deeply and sense the energy as they are sensing it.*
- ❖ *Breathe out once and open your eyes.*
- ❖ *Write down your experience.*

The Sacred Heart Exercise (4)

- ❖ *Move into the Heart (see <u>Moving into the Heart</u>).*
- ❖ *Breathe out once (let out a long, slow exhalation through your mouth).*
- ❖ *See, sense and feel all four chambers of the heart made of light; sense all blood vessels becoming brilliant shiny channels that carry rivers of light through you instead of organic blood.*
- ❖ *See how your heart made of light expands and gets bigger and bigger until all of you is within your heart.*
- ❖ *Feel that you yourself become light and lift up towards the Sun.*
- ❖ *See yourself in the Heart of The Sun.*
- ❖ *Now see yourself moving further into the Heart of The Universe.*
- ❖ *See, sense and feel yourself as part of the Fabric of The Universe; feel your responsibility in this universe and remember that responsibility is a gift, not a burden; be grateful for it.*
- ❖ *See and feel yourself being in multiple dimensions simultaneously.*
- ❖ *Breathe out once and open your eyes.*
- ❖ *Write down your experience.*

PART THREE
A Journey into the Heart

"If you lost heart in the Path of Love,
Flee to me without delay:
I am a fortress; invincible."

Rumi, D 17925

CHAPTER 8

The Heart: Door to the Center of the Universe

T here have been a couple of times when I have felt stars and galaxies, nebulae and interstellar clouds within my heart. How can that be possible?" I asked the Masters.

"The heart is literally a door to the Universe," revealed Tenzin Dhargey. "Once you start feeling your Heart energy and you realize that you can truly live from within your heart, your life is then changed forever."

"Once you move into your heart," continued Karma Dorje, "you will find a real place; actually it is more real than this world in the sense that this world was created there: in the heart!"

I probably had a perplexed expression on my face, as both masters smiled.

"Do not be confused, dear Tenzin," said Tenzin Dhargey. "Remember that inside your physical heart, there is a special place that those who are able to stay there call it the 'Place of Creation'. This place is the actual 'control room' of everything you do. Even if you think that there is a 'control room' inside your brain, it is merely a temporary movement of your consciousness, until you are able to come back to the heart."

"The funny thing is that people think that the brain gives orders to the heart; in fact it is the opposite," observed Karma Dorje.

"Is there anything written or documented about such an important subject?" I asked the Masters.

"All holy books provide a clear indication of the significance of the heart and how important it is to live from there," said Karma Dorje. "I remember when I visited a Greek community in America and had the opportunity of reading a huge book within a couple of days that is related to the monastic culture of Orthodox Christianity. I am not sure how well the English translation compared to the original texts that originate since the 4th century, but one thing is for certain: in this book, I read a clear indication about heart and how to get there."

"I assume you are referring to 'Philokalia'," I remarked.

"Yes, that's true," Karma Dorje replied.

"So the 'Moving into the Heart' meditation is probably the most important technique that you have shown me, isn't it?" I asked the Masters.

"Yes it is, dear Tenzin," Karma Dorje replied.

"And how can I get to that special place you speak of?" I asked curiously.

"Very easily." said Tenzin Dhargey. "Just let your intuition guide you from within the heart. Sooner or later, you will arrive there. For some it takes a moment; for others it takes a lifetime. It depends on your prior spiritual experience. In your case, you should get there in not time."

"Can I try doing it now? Would you help me?" I asked the Masters.

"Yes, of course," Tenzin Dhargey replied.

We started the meditation and after a while I heard Karma Dorje's warm voice say, "Move into the heart, dear Tenzin."

After I closed the door of the heart, Karma Dorje continued his instructions. It was as if we were doing this journey together.

"Now look around you," he instructed.

I seemed to be walking in a different world, within me. I was aware of being in my heart, but at the same time I realized that my heart was just an entry into a different dimension. I could see, sense and feel everything around me in a much better way than in my real body when I was walking into the Earth.

I could clearly see a night sky and stars around me, but suddenly I realized that I was literally floating in the Universe amongst the stars.

"Now use your intention and focus on the Place of the Creation," I heard Karma Dorje's voice say as if from light years away. The whole Universe was speaking through his voice.

Before I even finished placing my intention on this thought, a giant force suddenly pulled me through the Universe. Millions of light years passed by me in a flash; I could see, sense and feel billions of worlds passing through me, as well as myself through them. It felt really good; I experienced a strange pleasure, as if ancient and forgotten, taking me back to the source. And then, unexpectedly, I stopped. Strangely enough, I saw myself back in my childhood. My grandfather was holding my hand smiling at me. Near him were also both the Masters, smiling too. Tears of happiness streamed down my cheeks. I looked at my small hands and realized that I was probably around 4 or 5 years old. I clearly remembered that I had dreamt about this trip back then.

"So did this happen when I was four years old or is it happening now?" I asked the Masters with my sweet, childish voice.

"Does it really matter, dear Tenzin?" Karma Dorje replied looking at me, the small child.

"If it is of any importance to you," said Tenzin Dhargey, "it happened simultaneously, both times: then and now. I know this is hard for you to comprehend, but yes, it is possible to function in different times, at the same time. Remember. Everything is relative and fluid, isn't it?"

"How long can I stay here?" I asked the Masters.

"As long as you wish, dear Tenzin," Karma Dorje replied.

"Now we'll let you enjoy some time with your grandfather and when you want to come back to the Earth, we will be there," Tenzin Dhargey said.

I turned back to look at my grandfather and he smiled at me. When I looked behind me to see the Masters, nobody was there.

I had a hearty and warm chat with my grandfather. It was good for me to know that, after he had passed away few years ago, he was so happy on the other side of the Universe.

After a while I gently opened my eyes. Tears were still flowing down on my cheeks.

"So, am I able to see anybody that is not here anymore in the Place of Creation?" I asked the Masters.

"Yes, you can see anybody from any place and at any time," Tenzin Dhargey confirmed.

I sat for a while in silence and contemplated on the powerful experience that I had just gone through. I intuitively knew that this exercise had the capacity to change humanity.

I waited patiently until the Masters returned, as I wanted to ask them more questions about this exercise.

"I felt that you helped me get to the Place of Creation. Is this exercise easy for anyone to do on this planet or is a Master necessary to give a gentle 'push'?" I asked the Masters.

"Once you feel the vibration of your heart, it becomes very easy, dear Tenzin," Karma Dorje confessed.

"Those who live from the heart," said Tenzin Dhargey, "will, sooner or later, take the journey to the Place of Creation. It is a call that comes to all beings, whether human or non-human, who achieve the state of living from the heart or, in the case of non-humans, a similar heart-energy."

CHAPTER 9

The Heart: Healthiest Organ
of the Human Body

Is the heart the most important organ in the human body?" I asked the Masters.

"All organs are important, dear Tenzin," Karma Dorje replied. "How can it be possible to live without a liver or lungs or kidneys? How can one survive without a brain? However, the heart has a specific role owing to its enormous energy. By far, of all the organs, the heart has the largest energy field. Due to this huge energetic field of energy, the heart has some advantages over the other organs; for example, the heart will never get cancer."

"That's true," I exclaimed amazed by this revelation. "What is it about this cancer that we cannot comprehend?" I asked the Masters considering the ravages and damages caused by this illness.

"Dear Tenzin, first and foremost you must understand that all of us have dead cells in our bodies," explained Tenzin Dhargey. "Our body is a giant regenerator that continuously replenishes the cells. Apart from the first eight cells located in the coccyx bone, that never die, the rest of the cells, trillions and trillions of cells, are refreshed and reborn within. When a group of these cells are not eliminated and grow out of control then you have cancer cells that can dramatically affect the evolution of the body."

"Surprisingly, cancer and a lot of diseases can be easily prevented by what you eat and drink," Karma Dorje continued. "When I visited the western world, I found out that you have a way to measure your body's acidity or alkalinity. The pH is a measure of it. What the doctors told me is that if we have a pH less than 7 we have an acidic body; if the pH is greater than 7, then we have alkaline bodies. Well, it is very simple: cancer cannot survive in an alkaline environment. So, basically you need to watch what you eat."

"We came across some wonderful green vegetables in the western countries and they are sufficient to keep your body balanced and cancer free: broccoli, cucumber, celery, avocado, leafy greens, almonds, and so on. Some also grow kale and spinach. The most important element, though, is natural water from the springs. Drinking natural water straight from nature gives us the most powerful antidote against any illness!" Tenzin Dhargey said.

"That's true; we eat a lot of saturated fats, sugars, sodium and chloride," I agreed. ""There are already a lot of people out there who are suffering; how can they flush out their toxins?".

"Cleaning the body is greatly related to the liver. The liver is the cleaner of the body. Cleaning the liver is very easy. You have out there something that we don't have here; a magical fruit: lemon. Prepare a glass with natural water mixed with natural lemon juice, without adding any sugar, and drink it every single morning. Avocados and garlic are very healthy too, as well as, excellent liver cleaners. So are herbs, thyme, cilantro, including spice; turmeric is the best," Karma Dorje replied, demonstrating his knowledge of the human body.

"Remember what we've told you: the liver cannot handle more than four elements. When you eat a single piece of bread, see how many elements there are: water, salt, flour, yeast; at least four elements. So, another way to clean your liver is fasting or drinking only on water and natural juices," continued Karma Dorje.

"I have been a vegetarian," I said, "not even eggs and cheese, for a long time. A lot of people talk about avoiding eating animal products: meat, eggs and dairy products. I've heard a lot of discussions about these types of food being dangerous for the heart. I see that you barely eat and when you do, you either have a little salad or just some tea."

"Eating just vegetables is very healthy," explained Tenzin Dhargey. "Our stomach is not made to digest meat, dear Tenzin. It is also very important to remember that, whenever you eat meat, that piece of meat incorporates and includes the emotional energies of the animal. Your stomach digests the meat and your emotional body digests emotional energies from the animal. You will be charged and filled with all the tension and suffering that the animal has gone through. In fact, these charges are what affect and upset your heart."

"In a similar way," Karma Dorje continued, "your heart energy is affected by the energies of your partner when you have a sexual relationship. It is not just a simple act of reproduction. Let me explain it to you in another way. All the people with whom you have a sexual relationship, leave energies in your emotional bodies that affect your energy, your heart and the right side of your brain: the side that is directly related to the emotional body."

"Can these energies be transmitted from one person to another? If a man or a woman has had sexual relationships with a hundred people and somebody has a sexual relationship with that man or woman, is this person taking over all the energies of the one hundred people just through one sexual relationship?" I asked.

"It does not work like that," Karma Dorje answered smiling. "The emotional body is not mathematics and logic, dear Tenzin. Obviously that person is going to be affected, but not in the sense that he or she is receiving the energies of those one hundred people."

"Even when you hug somebody, it is not just a physical touch," Tenzin Dhargey explained. "Your mental and emotional bodies are exchanging messages. Your energies intertwine and mix together in an alchemical union, in a combination and a creation exercise. Hugging is healing. The simple good gesture and intention to hug generates enough energy to clean your bodies. The whole structure of the human body gets a refreshing jolt of light and energy. Your heart re-invigorates, revitalizes and fortifies with a fresh stream of prana and pure energy."

CHAPTER 10

The Heart: Coordinator of our Body's Energies

How are our hearts related to the energy of the Universe?" I asked the Masters.

"All the organs are related to the Universe's energy or to Prana, dear Tenzin," explained Tenzin Dhargey, "but our hearts have a specific role of transmitting energy further inside and outside our bodies. There is a big field of energy created by our hearts around us which keeps our bodies fresh and alive. It is like a vortex, a rotating field that moves out from the heart and "washes" and cleans all the organs, bones, muscles and it goes deeper, cleaning our channels of energies that cross our bodies. These are the energetic meridians."

"Try to think of it in this way: our hearts are the generators and main receivers of energy," said Karma Dorje. "If we truly live from within our hearts, they know when, where and how to send energy inside and outside of our bodies, in order to protect us. Try to see our hearts as our "speakers" on our behalf; see our hearts connected and speaking with each other even if, on the outside, we speak nonsense."

"Imagine that a being in this Universe has a center inside that is similar to our hearts," continued Tenzin Dhargey. "This center is a receiver and converter of any message coming from a similar 'device'."

"Try to figure out all the infinite number of hearts all over the Universe, all connected through thin, but powerful, threads of light," Karma Dorje said.

I closed my eyes for a moment and felt the infinite net of threads of light that connected our hearts. I saw myself and instantly knew that I am part of this huge cosmic fabric of light and love.

With my intention, I sent a message of love and compassion from my heart through this net just as if I would throw a small pebble in a lake and create small waves. I could literally see the millions of thin threads vibrate and light-up from my message of love and compassion.

What was more amazing, though, was that after a few seconds, I could see the threads vibrating back to me with a very powerful intensity. My heart filled with love and gratitude that came from the Universe. I was in awe and admiration and felt a reverential respect for our perfect hearts. I realized that we are love generators: the more we give, the more we receive. Actually we receive much more than we give.

I opened my eyes and looked at the Masters with respect and gratitude.

"It is nice to give and offer, dear Tenzin, isn't it?" Tenzin Dhargey smiled at me.

"Yes, it is, Master," I whispered with tears in my eyes.

"I understand that the heart is a perfect creation and a door to the Place of Light, but is there a Heart Imagery exercise that strengthens and fortifies the power of our hearts?" I asked the Masters.

"Yes, there is an ancient Heart Imagery exercise that draws more energy and light into the heart. Let's do it together." replied Karma Dorje.

The Hands of Light Exercise

- ❖ *Move into the Heart (see <u>Moving into the Heart</u>).*
- ❖ *Breathe out once (let out a long, slow exhalation through your mouth).*
- ❖ *See, sense and feel that your left hand is pointing to the Earth and it is getting longer and longer, going down through the Mother Earth and touching the middle of the Earth, the core of the Earth.*
- ❖ *See how your left palm is touching the energy and light from the core of the Earth and that it is filling up with light, being made of light.*
- ❖ *Keep your left hand down towards the core of the Earth and switch your attention to your right hand that is pointing to the sky.*
- ❖ *See how your right hand is getting longer and longer and it is going up through the sky to the Sun; it is getting even longer and it is touching the center of the Sun.*
- ❖ *Watch how your right palm is receiving light and energy from the Sun and it is filling up with light, being made of light.*
- ❖ *See now that both your hands are being made of light; the left hand is touching the center of the Earth and the right hand is touching the centre of the Sun.*
- ❖ *Now watch both your hands returning back to you in their normal size, but the palms remain filled with light and energy.*
- ❖ *Now place both palms over your heart and see and feel how your heart is filling up with light.*
- ❖ *See another place in your body where your energy is depleted or you have a wound and place your palms there, feeling the positive effect coming from the light.*
- ❖ *Breathe out once and open your eyes.*
- ❖ *Write down your experience.*

I opened my eyes and my heart had literally filled with light.

"Wow, this is a wonderful exercise" I exclaimed with enthusiasm.

"Yes, it is a good exercise not just for your heart but for any problem that you sense in your body" Tenzin Dhargey told me.

PART FOUR

History of Heart Imagery and Primary Exercises

"I sleep, but my heart waketh."

Song of Solomon, 5:2

Includes Revised & Updated Exercises from the previous book This Now is Eternity

CHAPTER 11

Introduction to the History of Heart Imagery

Today we will approach a very important subject. If you comprehend just a fraction of this, then your level of consciousness will be on the highest level of achievement! It regards Heart Imagery - Snying Gnasjal," said Karma Dorje with an enigmatic smile.

"Yes, I vaguely remember speaking about it long time ago," I remarked, puzzled by this Master's statement.

"We will start a set of exercises that will take, more or less, a full month," said Karma Dorje. "By 'we', I refer to Tenzin, myself and your Higher Self. Some of the exercises will come from yourself; from your Higher Self. Later on, you will remember some of the most important exercises and you will help others, who are still sleeping, start their awakening process.

"Remember when we met that I told you that now you are asleep? You were always asleep. Actually, we are all dreaming; night and day; continuously."

"Are these exercises part of the Tibetan meditation tradition?" I asked curiously.

"Nothing of what we are teaching you is part of the Tibetan tradition!" Karma Dorje replied.

I definitely looked stupefied, as both Masters started laughing.

"Who do you think we are?" asked Tenzin Dhargey looking into my eyes.

"Tibetan Masters!" I mumbled completely puzzled by their question.

"Why Tibetan?" Karma Dorje asked. "Why do you call it a 'Tibetan tradition'? Do you believe that the place where you were born is related to the level of your consciousness? Do you not believe that all Masters of this world share the same teachings? Do not all of us teach the same thing?"

"I guess you do..." I answered.

"These exercises are older than Tibet itself, my dear Tenzin!" explained Tenzin Dhargey. "When the Material Son and Daughter of God, whom we call here Adam and Eve, came here to upgrade our DNA and our consciousness, the people who had remained after they had gone, started using Heart Imagery techniques. Heart Imagery was used primarily by the Violet Race or the Adamic Race and later by the Vedics and the Sumerians.

"The first descendants of Adam and Eve, the Adamic Race or the Adamsonites, preserved the Heart Imagery exercises and continued to use them for over seven thousand years.

"The centre of their civilization was near Kopet Dag, near the Caspian Sea, in Turkmenistan, close to Iran. There in the highlands of Kopet Dag, were the headquarters of the Adamic or Violet Race.

"Four different groups of the Adamic Race migrated from Kopet Dag: the first group went to the Americas, the second group migrated to Greece, to the Mediterranean Islands and the Middle East area; the third group went to India and Tibet, where they formed the Andite-Aryans. The fourth group went to Europe.

"The Andites had tried to preserve the Heart Imagery spiritual work for over fifteen thousand years in the basin of the Tarim River in Sinkiang and in the South in the highland regions of Tibet, where the Andites had moved to from the Mesopotamia area. The Tarim Valley had been the centre of the true Andite culture. They built their settlements there and entered into trade relations with the progressive Chinese in the East and with the Andonites in the North. Their spiritual systems took over whatever remained of these powerful imagery techniques and they used them to balance their energies and understand higher dimensions."

I was really surprised by this history lesson given to me by Tenzin Dhargey and Karma Dorje.

"How do you know all these details?" I asked curiously.

"We were there," Karma Dorje replied very matter-of-factly.

I was already intuitively aware of the fact that my Masters could do things that were beyond my comprehension. Suddenly, I felt that they were actually part of the group of Adamic Masters; I knew that they were more than just human.

"The exercises are very simple and efficient," explained Tenzin Dhargey. "The order of the exercises, in the manner they were given to us, is not by chance. Each set of exercises is related to your subtle energy and it moves it towards the right direction. The secret of these exercises, from the teacher's point of view, is to know when the human mind kicks in and starts chatting; when the logical part of the brain, the left side, starts interfering. As a teacher of these techniques you must be aware of this before it happens, in order to give the next exercise!

"We will work on exercises from the Heart Imagery system, night and day for the period of one month, continuously, until you have completely quietened your mind and remember who you really are. Years from now, you might be able to remember the most powerful exercises that influenced your energy, and you might want to share your knowledge with other people."

"You will understand that life and death are interrelated and that everything around us is just an image. You will understand that death helps you see beyond this life and see other dimensions. You will become so deeply aware of death, that the future will become your present."

"You will see death and life as part of the Universe's creation," concluded Tenzin Dhargey as he smiled at me."

"Before beginning the exercises," said Karma Dorje, "you will need to clean your main chakras again. We will use a soft chanting and some ancient mantras that will clean the energy of your chakras. You will also see colors, images, lights and other expressions of the main five chakras that your senses will be able to perceive."

"We call this meditation the '*Divine Chanting Meditation*' and we usually have some young monks in the background chanting in a very soft tone.

"When you go back into the world, you can use some soft meditation music that resonates with your heart."

Steps for the Divine Chanting Meditation

❖ *Move into the Heart (see <u>Moving into the Heart</u>).*

❖ *Place your attention on the first chakra at the base of your body, at your perineum. See a beautiful red color; the mantra word for this chakra is LAM. Chant the mantra LAM gently from your heart, until you feel it spreading throughout your body.*

❖ *Place your attention on the second chakra behind your navel and see a shining orange-yellow color; the mantra word for this chakra is VAM. Chant the mantra VAM gently from your heart, until you feel it spreading throughout your body.*

❖ *Place your attention on the third chakra behind the middle of your chest and see a nourishing green color like the grass in springtime; the mantra word for this chakra is YAM. Chant the mantra YAM gently from your heart, until you feel it spreading throughout your body.*

❖ *Place your attention on the fourth chakra in the middle of your forehead and see a deep dark blue or indigo color, like the night sky on a summer night. This is where the third eye is or the seat of your dreams and visions. The mantra word for this chakra is SHAM; chant the mantra SHAM gently from your heart, until you feel it spreading throughout your body.*

❖ *Place your attention on the fifth chakra on the top of your head and see a shining gold-white glowing light; this is the crown chakra or the seat of Divinity; the mantra word for this chakra is AUM. Chant the mantra AUM gently from your heart, until you feel it spreading throughout your body.*

I started practicing this meditation and I felt an instant relief of unsettled energies within my chakras. I felt how the vibration of my chanting was really cleaning all my bodies: the physical, the mental and the emotional body. While I chanted the mantras, the Masters were softly chanting the same words in divine union of their magnificent voices. I was always delighted by their soft and, at the same time, powerful voices when they chanted. Their voices would emanate a strange combination of alpha and theta waves that automatically put me into a meditation state.

"Could you tell me more about Heart Imagery? It seems such a simple, yet powerful spiritual system," I asked the Masters.

"Heart Imagery is an ancient spiritual system coming from the ancient times. The Tibetan, Sumerian and Vedic spiritual mystery schools have been using it for thousands of years. It is related to the highest number of Mystery Schools: 555. We will also talk about Sacred Numerology later on," Tenzin Dhargey said.

"Heart Imagery helps and teaches you to balance your mental, emotional and physical bodies and it harmonizes your energy. In the future, especially after December 21, 2012 when Mother Earth will change her energy from masculine to feminine, Heart Imagery will be the most important technique that one could do, in order to bring harmony inside and outside!

"Heart Imagery exercises offer a pure experience: they are a set of key exercises that open your ability to see, sense and feel other dimensions.

"Unlike other spiritual systems, Heart Imagery exercises create freedom from the illusions of ego created by the mind.

"It is that part, from your heart, that helps you become a Master; to develop the awareness within that brings light and love. Right now the master in your heart is asleep. And the mind, the servant, is playing the role of the master. And the servant is not even your servant; the servant is created by the outside world, it follows the outside world and its laws.

"Once you enlighten your awareness through Heart Imagery exercises, it burns up the whole slavery that the mind has created. You will become a Master of your own destiny.

"In Heart Imagery you learn to surrender yourself," said Karma Dorje. "You learn to allow your ego to disappear. It is a set of "minor surrenders" that prepare you for the major, the total surrender when you lose your ego and the flowing light and energy comes to you!"

"Mastering heart imagery techniques will open to you to the ability to see the light of the heart and feel the sound or the inner vibration," concluded Tenzin Dhargey as he searched my eyes to see if I had comprehended the importance of what they had just told me.

I guess I had a very serious and solemn expression on my face since both Great Masters started laughing.

"Above all, "advised Tenzin Dhargey, "remember that this is just a dream, dear Tenzin. Do not try to analyze everything you see or sense. Just let it be. Just let the effect of the image work inside you. Just smile and feel free, dear Tenzin. You will soon understand that you are formless within a form."

CHAPTER 12

Heart Imagery Exercises

During the month that followed, I could not honestly tell whether I was in a dream or in what we call 'reality'.

The images that the Masters or my Higher Self were giving me where so real that I had to ask myself a couple of times whether I was still there with them or if I had transported inside that image. I understood why the Masters had told me that I would feel the inner sound and see the inner light.

I had found the sound of silence. Somewhere between or during the exercises, I felt the sound of soundlessness and saw glimpses of divine light. I had lost all my fears. I realized that, during these exercises, I had the same feeling that I used to experience when I was just two or three years old and my mother would play with me. I was not afraid. I was a child playing with his mother; I had opened up and had become vulnerable; detached and without any worries. I was like a child again: innocent, pure, eternal and the universe was my home.

It is difficult to split or break the Heart Imagery techniques into categories, but I could say that there were three clear trends unfolding in the exercises given by the Masters.

The first one regards cleaning the past. There was a clear tendency towards this direction during the first week.

Then, we spent almost two weeks healing the body, the organs inside the body and emotional traumas.

And finally, during the last week, I was given exercises that purified my mind, my heart, my spirit and my soul. The purpose of these sets of exercises and meditations where to connect with divinity and achieve union with God.

Each time we had a group of exercises that we would do together; Tenzin Dhargey or Karma Dorje would give the exercise, but I could feel that both Masters were also practicing it. After that, we would have a practical exercise each evening that I would have to do alone, to practice for a couple of hours until the Masters came back and we would resume the practice with a new set of exercises and meditations.

Obviously, it is almost impossible for me to write down all the exercises that we did together with the Masters, but I will write at least some of the most important exercises and meditations that we did together. I will try my best to give clear explanations and descriptions for all three categories:

Heart Imagery
- *Cleaning the Past and Self-Renewal*
- *Healing and Emotional Clarity*
- *Union with God*

Some suggestions when you do the Heart Imagery exercises:

Close your eyes (it would be a good idea to use a sleeping mask), sit upright in a chair or in a half lotus posture (be comfortable). Breathe in 3 times through your nostrils and breathe out through your mouth; your hands should be open and the palms facing down.

In Heart Imagery, the shorter time you stay with an image, the more powerful the result will be. A Master in Imagery knows when the brain of the student is ready to kick-in and that is the moment when he gives another image that keeps the student in the heart and the brain quiet.

Be a child again; do not analyze what you see, sense or feel. Let it happen naturally.

If you wish to practice the exercises, you will need somebody else to read them to you; it is not advised to read them or learn them off by heart, because that is when your mind will take over. The exercises are actually designed to quieten your mind, your brain. It will not, therefore, work if you read them and practice them. Trying to remember them involves the left brain, the logical and mental body.

But even when somebody else reads the exercises to you, that person must feel when the logical side of your brain, when your mental body, has begun to take over.

I know for sure that, whenever the Masters gave me an exercise, they knew exactly when my mind kicked in. I felt they would always "read" and "see" me when I stopped using the imagery system.

They knew when to give me the next exercise.

The first exercise is to always move our spirit from the brain to the heart.

Moving into the Heart Exercise

- ❖ *Close your eyes.*
- ❖ *Breathe three times (draw in a normal breath and let out a long, slow exhalation through the mouth. As you do this, see all your problems, issues, concerns and internal conflicts going out and away); then breathe in and out normally.*
- ❖ *Imagine a spiral staircase going down from the middle of your brain to the middle of your chest.*
- ❖ *Go down the stairs.*
- ❖ *Step off the stairs and slowly turn to your left.*

❖ *There is a door there that goes into your heart (it can be any type of door you can imagine).*

❖ *Open the door and step inside your heart; remember to close the door behind you.*

❖ *For a moment see, sense and feel the power and love emanating from your heart.*

CHAPTER 13

Cleaning the Past and Self Renewal

The first set of exercises ("Cleaning the Past and Self-Renewal") helped me understand the Heart Imagery Mystery School and it helped me clean my past and rebirth myself.

We all carry unclean energy from the past. There is a lot of imprisoned energy within us that has been left over from others. If we do not release this energy, we will not be able to understand and move to a higher level of consciousness.

Have you ever asked yourself how much unclean energy you carry with you from your past? Or awaken to how much energy is imprisoned within you from others? Do you realize that, without this liberation of energy, you cannot fly to a higher level of consciousness? Have you ever tried to better understand and therefore let go of past?

Can you imagine who you truly are when you cleanse your past? Why are you merely dreaming? Why are your dreams so disturbing sometimes, even waking up to run to this 'reality' in order to escape a terrified night? What are you doing to clean these dreams and harmonize yourself?

From the enjoyable experience that Cleaning the Past and Self-Renewal exercises offer, you will discover that these are just a few questions that need answering.

Blue Cloud Exercise

❖ *Move into the Heart (see Moving into the Heart).*

❖ *Breathe out once (let out a long, slow exhalation through your mouth).*

❖ *See, sense and feel that you are an empty vessel. See, sense and feel that a blue cloud comes and it enters your body from the top of your head (as if you have an opening there): a pure blue light is inside you now.*

❖ *See how the blue colored cloud goes out of your body through your toes and fingers: in the beginning the color is not very pure, but after a few seconds it becomes clear and it is like the pure blue sky.*

❖ *Continue receiving the blue cloud inside you from the top of your head until you see, sense and feel that the color of the cloud that is going out of your body through your fingers and toes is exactly the same color as the cloud that had entered from the top of your head.*

❖ *Breathe out once.*

❖ *See, sense and feel that you are completely clean, inside and out, and that you are connected with the whole universe.*

❖ *Breathe out once and open your eyes.*

❖ *Write down your experience.*

Ocean Water Exercise

❖ *Move into the Heart (see Moving into the Heart).*

❖ *Breathe out once (let out a long, slow exhalation through your mouth).*

❖ *See, sense and feel that you are an empty vessel with an opening at the top.*

❖ *See, sense and feel that you are floating over the pure, clean blue transparent water of the ocean.*

❖ *Now go into the water. Feel the water enter your body and clean it; see, sense and feel that all you have inside is clean, pure water.*

❖ *Breathe out once.*

❖ *See, sense and feel that you and the water have become one; there is only water mass and the ocean and yourself are one.*

❖ *Breathe out once and open your eyes.*

❖ *Write down your experience.*

Mountain Rock Exercise

❖ *Move into the Heart (see Moving into the Heart).*

❖ *Breathe out once (let out a long, slow exhalation through your mouth).*

❖ *See, sense and feel that you are walking on a mountain trail.*

❖ *See that in front of you, right in the middle of the trail, is a big, giant rock.*

❖ *See, sense, feel and know that you can go through the rock; feel that you are walking through it.*

❖ *Breathe out once.*

❖ *See, sense and feel that you are leaving behind all your issues and problems inside the rock (one minute).*

❖ *See, sense and feel that, soon, you will have finished passing through the rock.*

❖ *You only have ten steps left to go: 10, 9, 8, 7, 6, 5, 4, 3, 2, 1.*

❖ *You have passed through the rock now.*

❖ *Breathe out once.*

❖ *What is the difference between entering the rock and after having passed through it?*

❖ *Breathe out once and open your eyes.*

❖ *Write down your experience.*

Schools Colleagues and Friends Cleaning Exercise

❖ *Move into the Heart (see Moving into the Heart).*

❖ *Breathe out once (let out a long, slow exhalation through your mouth).*

❖ *See, sense and feel that you are a little child with your childhood friends. If there is something to clean there, go ahead and clean it. If there are some children or friends who have trespassed or hurt you, forgive them. If you have hurt somebody, forgive yourself. Try to feel their energy from your perspective now. How do you feel?*

❖ *Breathe out once.*

❖ *See, sense and feel that you are in high school amongst your classmates. If there is something to clean there, go ahead and clean it. If there are some colleagues who have trespassed or hurt you, forgive them. If you have hurt anyone, forgive yourself. See, sense and feel their energy from your perspective now. Without judging, just feel their energy. How do you feel?*

❖ *Breathe out once.*

❖ *See, sense and feel that you are at University with your friends and course mates. If there is something to clean there, go ahead and clean it. Feel their energy.*

❖ *Breathe out once.*

❖ *See, sense and feel that you are with your friends and colleagues now. If there is something to clean there, go ahead and clean it. How do you feel and see their energy now?*

❖ *See, sense and feel that you are with your friends and colleagues in the future. If there is something to clean there, go ahead and clean it. How do you feel and see their energy now?*

❖ *See, sense and feel that you are one: the past, the present and the future are the same. The little child, the teenager, the adult and the future adult you will be, are all the same. How do you feel now?*

❖ *Breathe out once and open your eyes.*

❖ *Write down your experience.*

Cleaning the Room of the Mind Exercise

❖ *Move into the Heart (see Moving into the Heart).*

❖ *Breathe out once (let out a long, slow exhalation through your mouth).*

❖ *See, sense and feel that you are in a big, big room with hundreds of different sized boxes, similar to those in a warehouse. Each box represents one of your thoughts.*

❖ *Breathe out once.*

❖ *Look in front of you and realize that the room is infinite, it has no end; you cannot see the end.*

❖ *Breathe out once.*

❖ *See, sense and feel that on your left hand side is a big, giant hole, like a vacuum.*

❖ *With your intention, start the vacuum cleaner and see the boxes disappearing one by one into the hole. The vacuum increases the speed and nearly all the boxes have gone now.*

❖ *See, sense and feel now that the room is empty.*

❖ *How do you feel? Analyze how it feels to be empty, without thoughts.*

❖ *Breathe out once and open your eyes.*

❖ *Write down your experience.*

Cleaning Mother Earth Exercise

❖ *Move into the Heart (see Moving into the Heart).*

❖ *Breathe out once (let out a long, slow exhalation through your mouth).*

❖ *See, sense and feel you are a cleaner of Mother Earth.*

❖ *See, sense and feel that you have become enormous and that Mother Earth is in your hands.*

❖ *Breathe out once.*

❖ *See, sense and feel that you are on another planet and you have Mother Earth in your hands. Place her under beautiful, spring water.*

❖ *Clean all the dirt off Mother Earth. See the brown water coming off, until it becomes clean and until you see the beautiful oceans and mountains.*

❖ *Breathe out once.*

❖ *Take Mother Earth and put her back.*

❖ *Breathe out once.*

❖ *See, sense and feel now that you are on a clean planet. How do you feel?*

❖ *Breathe out once and open your eyes.*

❖ *Write down your experience.*

Air-Body exercise

❖ *Move into the Heart (see Moving into the Heart).*

❖ *Breathe out once (let out a long, slow exhalation through your mouth).*

❖ *See, sense and feel that you are dissolving into pure air.*

❖ *See, sense and feel that you are in the lungs of all people and animals.*

❖ *See, sense and feel that you are in plants; all over the planet.*

❖ *Now feel that the air has become dense and you and all the air particles get together and structure your body again.*

❖ *What is the difference between before, when you were just air, and now that you are a body?*

❖ *Breathe out once and open your eyes.*

❖ *Write down your experience.*

Gazing Exercise

❖ *Move into the Heart (see Moving into the Heart).*

❖ *Breathe out once (let out a long, slow exhalation through your mouth).*

❖ *See, sense and feel that you are in a beautiful meadow amongst trees and that you are sitting in a lotus posture, gazing at a crystal that is right in the middle of the meadow.*

❖ *See, sense and feel that the crystal is alive and ready to take over all your past issues, problems, worries and resentments.*

❖ *See, sense and feel that a river of light is standing between you and the crystal and, all your past issues, problems, worries and resentments, are moving and flowing from you to the crystal.*

❖ *See, sense and feel that the crystal is transmuting all negative energies; they have left you and they have changed into positive energies.*

❖ *See, sense and feel that the energies are coming back to you through the river of light and that you did not lose any energy.*

❖ *What is the difference between gazing at the crystal and now that you have you connected with it?*

❖ *Breathe out once and open your eyes.*

❖ *Write down your experience.*

Waterfall Exercise

❖ *Move into the Heart (see Moving into the Heart).*

❖ *Breathe out once (let out a long, slow exhalation through your mouth).*

❖ *See, sense and feel that you are an empty vessel under a waterfall that is cleaning all the impurities of your physical body; the pure water enters your body and cleans all your organs.*

❖ *Breathe out once.*

❖ *See, sense and feel that you are an empty vessel under a waterfall of light that is cleaning the energy inside and out of your body.*

❖ *Breathe out once.*

❖ *What is the difference between going under the waterfall and now that you have come out of the waterfall?*

❖ *Breathe out once and open your eyes.*

❖ *Write down your experience.*

The Desert Exercise

- ❖ *Move into the Heart (see Moving into the Heart).*
- ❖ *Breathe out once (let out a long, slow exhalation through your mouth).*
- ❖ *See, sense and feel that you are in the middle of the desert; you are sitting in a lotus posture.*
- ❖ *Feel the wind. Feel transparent. The sand is sifting through you and it is cleaning you. It is coming from the left, rotating around your emotional body and then it is going to your right, taking all your particles with it.*
- ❖ *See, sense and feel how the sand is changing color as it sifts through you, from yellow on your left side, to brownish after it has passed through you towards the right.*
- ❖ *Breathe out once and open your eyes.*
- ❖ *Write down your experience.*

The Planet Keeper Exercise

- ❖ *Move into the Heart (see Moving into the Heart).*
- ❖ *Breathe out once (let out a long, slow exhalation through your mouth).*
- ❖ *See, sense and feel that you are the keeper of all animals on this planet. You are the one who takes care of all the animals on this planet. Elephants, lions, fish, whales, dolphins. You are like a zookeeper, but there is no zoo, just Mother Earth. How do you feel?*
- ❖ *Breathe out once.*
- ❖ *See, sense and feel now that you are taking care of all plants, flowers and trees on this planet. How do you feel now?*
- ❖ *Breathe out once.*
- ❖ *See, sense and feel that you are the keeper of all landscapes; water, mountains, desert, continents, all stones, crystals. You are the keeper of all these forms. How do you feel?*
- ❖ *Breathe out once and open your eyes.*
- ❖ *Write down your experience.*

The Timekeeper of the Universe

❖ *Move into the Heart (see Moving into the Heart).*

❖ *Breathe out once (let out a long, slow exhalation through your mouth).*

❖ *See, sense and feel and know that you are walking on an infinite road. Just keep walking. How do you feel walking on this infinite road that has no end and no beginning? Whatever you experience is welcome.*

❖ *Breathe out once.*

❖ *See, sense and feel as if you are jumping from one planet to another. Jump from Earth to Mars, from Mars to Pluto, from Pluto to Jupiter, and then onto other planets. Feel this energy, as you are jumping from one planet to another, as you travel through the Universe. How do you feel?*

❖ *Breathe out once.*

❖ *See, sense and feel that you are the timekeeper of the Universe. In your left hand you are holding time, you have places where there is time. In your right hand, you have places where there is no time.*

❖ *How do you feel being the timekeeper? Do you feel balanced? Do you feel the energy? Left hand: time. Right hand: no time.*

❖ *Breathe out once and open your eyes.*

❖ *Write down your experience.*

The Body as a Flower Exercise

❖ *Move into the Heart (see Moving into the Heart).*

❖ *Breathe out once (let out a long, slow exhalation through your mouth).*

❖ *See, sense and feel that your body is a flower bud; your head is the bud of the flower. What do you experience?*

❖ *Now see, sense and feel in your body events, emotions and situations from your life. How does the flower react to this? For some events you might feel that the flower almost dries up and for some events the flower glows in light and emanates a pleasant fragrance.*

❖ *Breathe out once.*

❖ *See, sense and feel that all humanity has become like what you are now: flower buds. And that the whole humanity senses its events and emotions as you are doing now.*

❖ *Feel that, after we get over all our emotions, then all of us, all the flowers, are glowing in light and we are like a planet with nice, beautiful, flowers*

❖ *Breathe out once and open your eyes.*

❖ *Write down your experience.*

The House Exercise

❖ *Move into the Heart (see Moving into the Heart).*

❖ *Breathe out once (let out a long, slow exhalation through your mouth).*

❖ *See, sense and feel that you are in front of a house and you know that inside the house you have manifested all past angers, frustrations and resentments. Go inside the house and start cleaning it. Take a broom and clean the floor, take the dust, paint the walls in your favorite colors.*

❖ *Breathe out once.*

❖ *Now go outside and clean the garden and turn the exterior of the house into the way you would like it to be.*

❖ *Go inside the house again, place a comfortable chair near the window and sit there looking outside.*

❖ *How do you feel now that you have cleaned the house?*

❖ *Breathe out once and open your eyes.*

❖ *Write down your experience.*

Practical exercises that can be used in our daily activities without meditation

"Switch" your Energy Exercise

This exercise is to be done first with a Heart Imagery Teacher, in order to understand how to switch the energy.

When you get into a reaction, into a secondary instinct, try to recognize the emotion which the basic energy has transformed into and has now become a secondary instinct. For example: you may have become depressed (emotion) and have gone to sleep upset and angry (secondary instinct).

When you feel that the energy is changing into an emotion (depression), as soon as you feel the first signs of the emotion in you, switch your energy to harmony: see the word 'HARMONY' written with golden letters in front of you and visualize that you are in harmony.

What image do you have for being in harmony? Perhaps you see that you are sitting in a lotus posture in meditation or that you are sitting quietly in a park quietly, enjoying nature or up in the mountains, in the middle of a forest of cedar trees with a spring water nearby.

Water Exercise

Pour water into a glass and keep the glass in your hands for 10 seconds while focusing all your attention on the water.

With your intention, send light and love to the water from your heart through your hands directly to the water and say to the water 3 times: "I love you".

See, sense and feel that the water has become structured and alive.

Drink the water slowly and, as you swallow it down, say to the water 3 times: "I love you, I love you, I love you".

Stop and Breathe exercise

Remember to STOP 3 times a day from whatever you are doing (computer, work, shopping, watching TV) just for 10 seconds and remember to breathe: take 3 long inhalations through your nostrils and 3 long exhalations through your mouth.

We have habits and we need to take a pause from them. We need to make some time to return to our bodies each day.

Clean the Dreams Exercise

Remember that whatever you dream of, is your truth; it has been created by yourself. Do not blame somebody else for your dreams, because you are the one who has created them.

How to clean your nightmares or the dreams that make you feel uncomfortable:

The first step is to understand your dreams. You cannot understand a dream while you are sleeping, because you are in the dream.

So first program yourself, before falling asleep, to remember the dream.

In the morning when you wake up, take each dream and meditate. Do not be afraid. Go back into the dream. Remember that fear is there to teach you courage.

Clean the dream: if you have dreamt a house that is dirty and messy, then clean the house, clean it all; clean the dream until you feel happy, calm, relaxed.

Unnecessary Repetitions

Unnecessary Repetitions are a big alarm for your energy. Check yourself. Whenever you do one of these unnecessary repetitions, you lose energy.

Do you perhaps have bell-words, such as "whatever" or any other words? Do you have any specific tics, like twirling your hair or scratching your head when somebody asks you a difficult question? Find them all and be aware when you tend to do each one.

At the beginning you will be caught by the habit of saying it or doing it, but in time you will do it less and less.

When you stop all the unnecessary repetitions, you will no longer be tired. Instead, you will feel fresh and you will have enough energy to get through the day.

CHAPTER 14

Healing and Emotional Clarity

H*eart Imagery - Healing and Emotional Clarity-* is one of the most important steps in healing your Mental Body, Emotional Body and Physical Body. It gives you power to go beyond the belief patterns that keep your mind blocked. It gives you tools to clean your emotional traumas that are moving your energies inside and outside in a wrong manner.

One of the most fundamental things to remember is that, whatever illness affects your physical body is just a consequence of your belief patterns and your emotional trauma. Even great meditators cannot go into their inner journey without cleaning their mental body and emotional body.

Do you understand how important it is to clean your energies? An awakened spirit needs this experience. The more you continue doing these exercises, you will experience the silence beyond belief patterns and beyond emotional issues; a small flame of awareness is burning inside.

The Sun Exercise

- ❖ *Move into the Heart (see <u>Moving into the Heart</u>).*
- ❖ *See yourself sitting outside in a garden or in a park in the morning at the time of the day when the sun is up at the level of your forehead.*
- ❖ *See, sense and feel that the warmth and the light of the Sun have reached you.*
- ❖ *See, sense and feel the Sun coming slowly, slowly to your head, your forehead. The Sun is entering right through the middle of your forehead and it is now inside your head.*
- ❖ *Turn your eyes inwards and see the Sun inside your head.*
- ❖ *Breathe out once.*
- ❖ *See the Sun coming slowly down through your throat, powerfully lighting up your throat.*
- ❖ *See the Sun coming slowly down and inside your upper chest area, shining powerfully in that entire area.*
- ❖ *See the Sun coming slowly down to your lower chest area, warming it all up.*
- ❖ *See the Sun coming slowly down to your stomach area.*
- ❖ *See the Sun coming slowly down to your abdomen area, warming it all up.*
- ❖ *Breathe out once.*
- ❖ *See, sense and feel that the warmth and the light of the Sun are going inside your kidneys and from there up through your spine. The spine is like a tree and the light is going around the spine from left to right, exactly like the branches of a tree.*
- ❖ *Breathe out once and open your eyes.*
- ❖ *Write down your experience.*

The Moon Exercise

- ❖ *Move into the Heart (see <u>Moving into the Heart</u>).*
- ❖ *See yourself sitting outside in a garden or in a park in the evening when the Moon is up shining in a beautiful night sky.*
- ❖ *See, sense and feel that the white light of the Moon is coming to you.*
- ❖ *See, sense and feel that the Moon is coming slowly, slowly down to your feet, in front of you. The Moon is entering right through the soles of your feet.*
- ❖ *See, sense and feel that the white, clear light of the Moon is cleaning out your right foot and your left foot.*
- ❖ *See, sense and feel that the light of the Moon is going up, cleaning your right knee and your left knee.*
- ❖ *See, sense and feel that the white light of the Moon is going up, cleaning your right hip and your left hip.*
- ❖ *Breathe out once.*
- ❖ *See, sense and feel that the sparkling white light of the Moon is going up from your hips to your spine, all over your body and your organs. The spine is like a tree and the light is going around the spine from left to right, exactly like the branches of a tree.*
- ❖ *Breathe out once and open your eyes.*
- ❖ *Write down your experience.*

The Lake Exercise

- ❖ *Move into the Heart (see <u>Moving into the Heart</u>).*
- ❖ *See, sense and feel that you are floating on a lake on a beautiful night, facing up towards a clear sky, and that you see thousands of stars.*
- ❖ *See, sense and feel that the sky is mirrored in the lake and seven stars are mirrored directly onto your chakras.*
- ❖ *See how your seven chakras are shining and are cleaned by the seven stars.*

❖ *Now see that you are moving up to the sky and the real stars are mirrored in your transparent body; see the lake and the stars down onto the lake; feel that you are in both places now: on the lake and in the sky.*

❖ *Gently let yourself move back from the sky and connect with your physical body.*

❖ *How do you feel now?*

❖ *Breathe out once and open your eyes.*

❖ *Write down your experience.*

Lighting your Organs Exercise

❖ *Move into the Heart (see <u>Moving into the Heart</u>).*

❖ *See, sense and feel that the Sun is becoming smaller and smaller and that it is coming right in front of you at the level of your chest; the Sun is like a small sphere with a diameter of 20 cm.*

❖ *See, sense and feel that your heart is traveling outside of your body right near the small Sun that is in front of you; now your heart is moving inside the small sun and it is filling up with light (wait 30 seconds). Now your heart, that is full of light, is moving back into your body, back to her location; the light is shining from your heart throughout your entire chest area (wait 30 seconds).*

❖ *Breathe out once.*

❖ *See, sense and feel that your liver is traveling outside of your body, right near the small Sun that is in front of you; now your liver is moving inside the small sun and it is filling up with light (wait 30 seconds). Now your liver is full of light and it is moving back into your body, back to its location; the light is shining from your liver throughout the stomach-liver area (wait 30 seconds).*

❖ *Breathe out once.*

❖ *See, sense and feel that your kidneys are traveling outside of your body right near the small Sun that is in front of you; now your kidneys are moving inside the small sun and they are filling up with light (wait 30 seconds). Now your kidneys are full of light and they are moving back into your body back to their location; the light is shining from your kidneys throughout the lower back abdominal area (wait 30 seconds).*

❖ *Breathe out once.*

❖ *See, sense and feel that your lungs are traveling outside of your body right near the small Sun that is in front of you; now your lungs are moving inside the small sun and they are filling up with light (wait 30 seconds). Now your lungs are full of light and they are moving back into your body back to their location; the light is shining from your lungs throughout the upper chest area (wait 30 seconds).*

❖ *Breathe out once.*

❖ *See, sense and feel that your brain is traveling outside of your body right near the small Sun that is in front of you; now your brain is moving inside the small sun and it is filling up with light (wait 30 seconds). Now your brain is full of light and it is moving back into your body back to its location; the light is shining from your brain throughout your head area (wait 30 seconds).*

❖ *Now see yourself with your heart, liver, kidneys, lungs and brain shining inside you.*

❖ *How do you feel?*

❖ *Breathe out once and open your eyes.*

❖ *Write down your experience.*

Lotus Flower Exercise

❖ *Move into the Heart (see <u>Moving into the Heart</u>).*

❖ *See, sense and feel a Lotus flower right ahead of you, towards the middle of your forehead, at the level of your third eye. Now the Lotus flower is getting bigger and bigger until you sit on it.*

❖ *See, sense and feel that the Lotus flower is beginning to move upwards, while you are sitting on it; look down and see the buildings, the trees, all the area around; go higher and higher until you are between white clouds that are floating near you.*

❖ *Now move back to the room.*

❖ *Breathe out once.*

❖ *See, sense and feel that the Lotus flower is getting smaller and smaller and it is moving down to your first chakra at your perineum level; your first chakra is shining and it is emanating a pleasant fragrance.*

❖ *See, sense and feel that the Lotus flower is moving up towards your navel chakra right there in the middle of your body, behind the belly button. Your navel chakra is shining and it is emanating a pleasant fragrance.*

❖ *See, sense and feel that the Lotus flower is moving up towards your upper heart chakra right there in the middle of the chest; your heart chakra is shining and it is emanating a pleasant fragrance.*

❖ *See, sense and feel that the Lotus flower is moving up towards your third eye chakra; your third eye chakra is shining and it is emanating a pleasant fragrance.*

❖ *See, sense and feel that the Lotus flower is moving up towards your crown chakra; your crown chakra is shining and it is emanating a pleasant fragrance.*

❖ *Now see, sense and feel that the Lotus flower is getting bigger and bigger and again and you are sitting on it; how do you feel now?*

❖ *Breathe out once and open your eyes.*

❖ *Write down your experience.*

Emotional Body Exercise

❖ *Move into the Heart (see <u>Moving into the Heart</u>).*

❖ *See, sense and feel that your spirit is moving outside and up above your body up and over your own Leonardo sphere.*

❖ *Look down and see your emotional body as a cloud around you and it is spinning clockwise; your emotional body is inside your Leonardo sphere.*

❖ *With your intention, send light down to your emotional body from up where your spirit is looking down; see, sense and feel how your emotional body, like a vortex, is receiving light inside from up there, and it is cleaning all the energies that do not correspond with your emotional body's energy.*

❖ *Breathe out once.*

❖ *See, sense and feel that your emotional body is becoming a white shining cloud around your physical body; feel calm and clean; your emotional traumas are cleaned.*

❖ *Move your spirit back.*

❖ *Breathe out once and open your eyes.*

❖ *Write down your experience.*

Waterfall of Light Exercise

❖ *Move into the Heart (see <u>Moving into the Heart</u>).*

❖ *See that you are sitting in front of two beautiful and serene mountains; in the middle of these two mountains is a waterfall of light.*

❖ *See that you are getting closer and closer to the waterfall, until you arrive in front of it.*

❖ *Now step right under the waterfall of light and see, sense, feel and know that the light is cleaning your mental and emotional bodies that are around your physical body.*

❖ *When the light begins to clean your mental and emotional bodies, feel that your brain is getting cleaner and that you are receiving clarity and peace; know that your mental body is linked with the left brain and your emotional body is linked with the right brain.*

❖ *Stay there for a minute and feel the light cleaning your bodies and filling your brain with clarity.*

❖ *Breathe out once and open your eyes.*

❖ *Write down your experience.*

The Seven Components of Healing Exercise

❖ *Move into the Heart (see <u>Moving into the Heart</u>).*

❖ *See, sense and feel that, here on Earth, we have seven magical components that we may use to heal: energy, movement, water, light, sound, Mother Earth and flowing time.*

❖ *Know that energy is everything and everything is energy. You are, therefore, able to heal yourself with energy.*

❖ *Know that energy always moves and that life is movement; we are not static; we move and, when we move, the energy moves and heals us.*

❖ *Know that we are primarily made of water, so if we clean out the water from inside us, by bringing in clean water, we are able to heal ourselves.*

❖ *Know that light or fire guided by our will and our intention cleans our chakras and heals us.*

❖ *Know that sound heals; right now, listen to your "inner sound" and let it expand throughout your being; feel how the vibration of the sound heals you.*

❖ *Know that connection with Mother Earth heals; see, sense and feel the healing energy coming from Mother Earth in all your cells; feel that you have to honor who you are as part of Mother Earth; as part of Nature.*

❖ *Know that eternal time is liquid, it flows; see, sense and feel that without time you are eternal; healing happens instantly when you realize that you are eternal.*

❖ *Breathe out once and open your eyes.*

❖ *Write down your experience.*

Message from your Ancestors Exercise

❖ *Move into the Heart (see <u>Moving into the Heart</u>).*

❖ *See, sense and feel that you are walking on a serene mountain trail. You remember this trail, as if you have been there before. Listen to the song of the birds around you. Spring water is flowing down near* the trail. Kneel and drink the pure and refreshing water. Wash your eyes with this water.

❖ *There is a cave right there in front of you; enter the cave and remember when you used to meditate here in your past lives. Feel the connection with this holy place and start meditating there, sitting on a solid rock covered with an old rug.*

❖ *See, sense and feel the bond with the mountain and the Mother Earth.*

❖ *See, sense and feel the relationship with the sky and the Father Universe.*

❖ *See, sense and feel the link with the other workers of light from all over the world and from all over the Universe.*

❖ *Now ask your ancestors to come. Hear what they have to tell you. They give you a message that has to do with your mental body, emotional body and physical body. They tell you how to heal yourself. Hear this message.*

❖ *One by one, your ancestors leave and you remain there meditating on their message.*

❖ *See, sense and feel that it is time to let go of any places you have been in, in this existence and that you live only in the now. Feel that the past is over and you have a new energy. You are reborn again; ready to enjoy other beautiful experiences.*

❖ *Breathe out once and open your eyes.*

❖ *Write down your experience.*

Traveling the Universe Exercise

❖ *Move into the Heart (see <u>Moving into the Heart</u>).*

❖ *Start moving inside the Heart towards the opposite direction facing the door of the Heart.*

❖ *Shortly, you will arrive to the other side of your Heart, where you will see another door; open that door and step outside.*

❖ *See, sense and feel that you are in the Universe and that there is a road leading from your heart up to the Sun of our Solar System;*

> *take this road and move up towards the Sun; arrive at the Sun and move to the center of It.*

❖ *See, sense and feel that there is a road leading from the center the Sun to the Galactic Sun - the centre of our Galaxy; take this road and move towards the Galactic Sun; when you have reached the Galactic Sun see, sense and feel thousands of constellations on the left and right side of the road.*

❖ *See, sense and feel the Galactic Sun; an Archangel of Light is guiding you within this area towards the centre of the Galactic Sun, where the Council of our Galaxy is coordinating all the worlds and Suns; you have now arrived and the Council has a message for you. Hear their message.*

❖ *They also have a gift for you; take the gift with both hands and thank them for it. The Archangel is now taking you back to our Solar System Sun. From there, return to the door on your own and open the door. Go back into your Heart.*

❖ *See, sense and feel the importance of the message and the gift that you have received; put the gift down, sit down and begin to meditate.*

❖ *Breathe out once and open your eyes.*

❖ *Write down your experience.*

The Room Exercise

❖ *Move into the Heart (see <u>Moving into the Heart</u>).*

❖ *See that you are in a nice place, sitting in a lotus posture.*

❖ *Look around you, what do you see?*

❖ *Now see yourself sitting in a small dark room.*

❖ *Look around at the walls of that room. They are tough, dark, and impenetrable.*

❖ *How do you feel?*

❖ *Now see that the walls have been replaced by windows: big, huge, bright windows.*

❖ *There is no darkness any more. You can see the sky through these windows.*

❖ *See that the roof of the room has also become a window through which you can see white clouds in the sky.*

❖ *Now look downwards, where you are sitting. There is no floor any more, it has also been replaced by a window, from which you can see the blue sky.*

❖ *Feel the light that is shining in towards you.*

❖ *Feel the light that you are shining outwards.*

❖ *Breathe out once and open your eyes.*

❖ *Write down your experience.*

The Astral Spine Exercise

❖ *Move into the Heart (see <u>Moving into the Heart</u>).*

❖ *See that you are in a nice place, sitting in a lotus posture.*

❖ *See, sense and feel that your spine is transparent, like a tube of light.*

❖ *Now mentally place the word "OM" down at the base of the spine.*

❖ *Now move up with your attention and mentally put the word "OM" in the lumbar region, on the same level as the navel.*

❖ *Now move up with your attention and mentally put the word "OM" in the dorsal area, between the shoulder blades.*

❖ *Now move up with your attention and mentally put the word "OM" in the middle of the brain.*

❖ *Finally put the word "OM" up on top of your head.*

❖ *Feel two invisible strings of light moving up from the base of the spine to the middle of the brain: this is Pingala or the solar nerve on the right side of the spine and Ida or the lunar nerve on the left side of the spine.*

❖ *See, sense and feel how the solar nerve draws the esoteric fire up to your brain and how and the lunar nerve draws the esoteric silvery cold energy up, that is located at the base of the spine.*

❖ *Feel the blissful light in your brain.*

❖ *Breathe out once and open your eyes.*

❖ *Write down your experience.*

Practical exercises that can be used in our daily activities with or without meditation

Tibetan Chakra Cleaning Exercise

❖ *Move into the Heart (see <u>Moving into the Heart</u>).*

❖ *See yourself, your body there in front of you like a holographic image; see a ray of light extending from your palm chakra (it does not matter which hand) to the first chakra (base chakra) of your holographic image. Clean it with the light that is coming from your palm until you see, sense and feel a beautiful red color and a fragrance of roses coming from there.*

❖ *Move your palm upwards and clean the second chakra; it is located between the base chakra and the navel. Clean it until you see, sense and feel a beautiful orange color; feel the creation energy being cleaned and released. Feel the fragrance of the orange tree flowers.*

❖ *Move your palm upwards and clean the third chakra of your holographic image; it is located on the level of the solar plexus, of the stomach. Clean it until you see or feel a beautiful yellow color shining right there, like a small Sun inside your solar plexus. Feel the fragrance of the yellow lemon tree flowers.*

❖ *Now move your palm upwards and clean the fourth chakra; it is located in the middle of the chest area between lungs. Clean the upper heart chakra until you see or feel a beautiful nourishing green color shining right there. Feel the fragrance of the mint green leaves.*

❖ *Now move your palm upwards and clean the fifth chakra; it is located in the lower throat. Clean it until you see or feel a beautiful blue color, like a summer sky. Feel the fragrance of the linden tree flowers.*

❖ *Now move your palm upwards and clean the sixth chakra - the third eye; it is located in the middle of the forehead. Clean it until you see or feel a beautiful indigo. Feel the fragrance of the Lila flowers.*

❖ *Finally move your palm upwards and clean the seventh chakra - the crown chakra. Clean it until you see or feel a beautiful white color. Feel the fragrance of the jasmine flowers.*

❖ *See, sense and feel that all your chakras from both - your holographic image and your physical body - are cleaned and they are emanating a pleasant fragrance, like a garden of flowers.*

❖ *Now allow your hologram to merge with your physical body.*

Practical Exercise to Let go of Anxiety and Fears and Connect with your Inner Essence

❖ *Move into the Heart (see <u>Moving into the Heart</u>).*

❖ *Remember a situation when you were anxious, upset or afraid.*

❖ *Now observe the rhythm of your breath: the inflow and outflow of your breath; observe how you inhale and exhale without trying to change anything during this process.*

❖ *You may find that your breathing spontaneously becomes faster or slower, deeper or shallow and may even stop from time to time; allow all these changes to happen without resistance or anticipation.*

❖ *Whenever your attention moves back to the anxiety or the fear from that situation or a sensation in your body (for example whenever your heart beat increases), gently return your awareness to your breathing.*

❖ *In a minute or so you will calm down and pass the anxiety and the fear.*

The Spiral (Fibonacci) Interior Smile

❖ *Move into the Heart (see <u>Moving into the Heart</u>).*

❖ *Realize that inside your Heart is the center of the Universe and it forms a spiral of light that goes through your main organs in the following order: Heart, Left Lung, Brain, Right Lung, Liver, Right Kidney, Genitals, Left Kidney and Spleen. It then moves outwards continuing the spiral movement towards the infinite.*

❖ *Move your attention to your Heart and smile at your heart: practice the Interior Smile with your Heart while you say three times to your Heart: "I love you"; after a few seconds you will feel your Heart vibrating and smiling back at you.*

❖ *Now move your attention to your Left Lung and smile at your Left Lung: practice the Interior Smile with your Left Lung, while you tell your Left Lung three times "I love you"; after a few seconds you will feel how your Left Lung vibrates and smiles back to you.*

❖ *Now practice the Interior Smile with your Brain, Right Lung, Liver, Right Kidney, Genitals, Left Kidney and Spleen.*

❖ *See, sense and feel now that your nine organs are filled with love and light and that they are smiling back at you.*

❖ *Realize again that the center of the Universe is inside your Heart and it forms a spiral of light that goes through your main organs in the following order: Heart, Left Lung, Brain, Right Lung, Liver, Right Kidney, Genitals, Left Kidney and Spleen. It moves outwards continuing the spiral movement to the infinite. See and feel this spiral of light moving continuously from your Heart through your organs and proceeding outwards towards the infinite.*

Practice this exercise once a day or when you feel disconnected from your Higher Self and from the Universe; when you feel sad and alone.

The Tibetan Hands

Close your eyes.

❖ *Move into the Heart (see Moving into the Heart).*

❖ *Rub your hands for a minute relaxing your wrists without opening your eyes.*

❖ *Sense the parts of your body that are weaker, congested, depleted. Look for the painful areas or for the hot, cold, irregular tingling from electrical charges.*

❖ *Allow your hands to gently massage the areas of tension, making full contact. Be totally aware of the area of your body where your hands feel areas of tension.*

❖ *See, sense, feel and know that the white light travels from your hands to the area of pain or tension. See how the area of pain or tension has gradually turned into an area filled with white shining light.*

Cleaning With Prana

❖ *Move into the Heart (see <u>Moving into the Heart</u>).*

❖ *See, sense and feel how each cell of your body becomes an infinite small window opened to the Universe.*

❖ *Now inhale and feel how prana is coming inside your body, in all your cells through the opened windows.*

❖ *See, sense and feel how your entire body has filled with prana.*

❖ *See, sense and feel that your body is filled with prana now and that prana moves from your body to your Leonardo sphere; your Leonardo sphere is now a sphere of prana all around you.*

CHAPTER 15

Union with God

Karma Dorje told me once that God is very real for those who understand that God is within and without, inside and outside. Heart Imagery - Union with God exercises help us have an awareness of perfect Oneness. What could God give us, other than perfect knowledge of Himself? The belief that we could give and get something else, something outside ourselves, has cost us the awareness of Oneness and of our Identity.

If we practice these exercises correctly we should experience a sense of relaxation and the feeling that we are entering into the light. During the exercises, as we pass by the thoughts of this world, we will understand that God's light is formless and limitless and we will understand that none of what we think as our real thoughts are in any way similar to our real thoughts.

Because we are part of His Creation and Mind, our thoughts are part of His Mind.

These exercises help us find the place within us where there is perfect peace; there is a place in us where nothing is impossible. There is a place in us where the strength of God lives. There is nothing to fear.

Union with God is not an effect; it is a cause. We are created to be in union with the Universe and later it becomes the natural result of choosing right, free of guilt. This is so essential to spiritual learning that it should never be forgotten.

The Primary Source Exercise

❖ *Move into the Heart (see <u>Moving into the Heart</u>).*

❖ *Breathe out once (let out a long, slow exhalation through your mouth).*

❖ *See, sense and feel that you are traveling in space from here, from this location directly to the Primary Source.*

❖ *Know that the Primary Source is the source of all that is.*

❖ *How do you see the Primary Source? How does It appear in front of you?*

❖ *Try to see it, feel it and know it.*

❖ *See, sense and feel that Pure Knowledge is in front of you, but that what you see is given by your perception; realize that perception belongs to the world of duality, like our world. Pure Knowledge belongs to Primary Source.*

❖ *See, sense and feel that your perception has no function in the Primary Source, in God. However, the perception is very useful to you; it must become the means for the reinstatement of your awareness and holiness.*

❖ *Breathe out once.*

❖ *See, sense and feel that you are moving inside the Primary Source; how do you feel now?*

❖ *See, sense and feel that you cannot see anything other than the Primary Source, because you cannot be apart from the Primary Source, from God.*

❖ *Sense now how enriched you are and feel renewed and revitalized.*

❖ *Breathe out once and open your eyes.*

❖ *Write down your experience.*

The Healing Prayer Exercise

❖ *Move into the Heart (see <u>Moving into the Heart</u>).*

❖ *Breathe out once (let out a long, slow exhalation through your mouth).*

❖ *See, sense and feel that you are walking into a forest moving towards a distant light.*

❖ *Find that you are in an open space in the middle of the forest without trees; a light is coming from above and a perfect circle is formed on the ground.*

❖ *Stop right in the middle of the circle and feel the light coming from above.*

❖ *Standing in the middle of the circle, say a healing prayer; let your intuition and your Higher Self give you the words; do not think logically about the prayer nor try to remember any prayers that you know from the past. Allow any healing prayer you may feel like saying now to come to you naturally.*

❖ *End your prayer with the words: "So Be It".*

❖ *Breathe out once.*

❖ *See, sense and feel that your prayer has been heard by God.*

❖ *See, sense and feel that God's hands are coming from above into the circle of light and that they are lifting you up. Feel that, now as you are traveling up in the hands of God, healing is taking place (wait for 2 minutes).*

❖ *Now feel that God's hands are gently bringing you back to the center of the circle. Feel as if you have a new life, as if you are reborn again.*

❖ *Breathe out once and open your eyes.*

❖ *Write down your experience.*

Heart of Father Universe Exercise

❖ *Move into the Heart (see <u>Moving into the Heart</u>).*

❖ *Breathe out once (let out a long, slow exhalation through your mouth).*

❖ *See, sense and feel that you are now in the middle of the Universe, right in the Heart of the Universe. Feel how the Heart of the Universe is pulsating all around you; a soft and tender heart beat.*

❖ *See, sense and feel a point of light pulsating inside your heart; the point of light is expanding and contracting with strong rhythmic movements. Feel the waves of light generated by the point of light that is pulsating inside your heart; you can hear a rhythmical throbbing sound coming from the point of light that is pulsating inside your heart.*

❖ *Now gently feel how your pulsation and pulsation of the Heart of the Universe have unified and they have become one; feel the unity of the Hearts and feel only one Heart Beat. The point of light from your heart has connected with the Heart of the Universe.*

❖ *Breathe out once.*

❖ *See, sense and feel that you need to reach the level of total unity with every other person around you, in order to hear the Heart of God; try to bring into the Heart of the Universe all the people with whom you had a conflict or a disagreement and feel the difference between their heart beat and the beat of the Heart of the Universe.*

❖ *Help these people rise up to the same level of unity as you are on now and see, sense and feel them merge with the beat of your heart and of the Heart of the Universe.*

❖ *See, sense and feel that now you are all one person with one heart.*

❖ *Breathe out once and open your eyes.*

❖ *Write down your experience.*

Cleaning with Colors Exercise

❖ *Move into the Heart (see <u>Moving into the Heart</u>).*

❖ *Breathe out once (let out a long, slow exhalation through your mouth).*

❖ *See, sense and feel your favorite color like a cloud right in front of you. Feel this color coming towards you from the left, like the wind; feel it going through you, cleaning your emotional body. Now feel an opposite color (whatever an opposite color means to you) coming from the right side, cleaning your mental body. Now feel both colors coming from both directions, going through you, cleaning you completely.*

❖ *See, sense and feel that you can help clean all your friends, all humanity. Send this two-colored wind from left to right across the planet, cleaning all people on its path. Now send it from the right, cleaning all humanity. Now send it from both sides at once.*

❖ *See, sense and feel that you are in the middle of the universe; there are stars all around you.*

❖ *See, sense and feel that there is a giant vacuum cleaner on your left hand side that is taking in all your emotions, issues and negative thoughts. They all go to your left in this vacuum cleaner.*

❖ *Breathe out once and open your eyes.*

❖ *Write down your experience.*

The Color of God Exercise

❖ *Move into the Heart (see <u>Moving into the Heart</u>).*

❖ *Breathe out once (let out a long, slow exhalation through your mouth).*

❖ *See, sense and feel that you are on the edge of a mountain and feel that it is the end of time. How does it feel? What does "end of time" mean to you? End of time could mean an end to anything, such as going into a new dimension or entering a new relationship, anything at all.*

❖ *Breathe out once.*

❖ *See, sense and feel the Color of God. How does the Color of God appear to you? This color is approaching you like a cloud, it envelopes you and it enters into you. You become this color. Your stomach, liver, eyes, mental and emotional bodies are this color. Your physical body is this color.*

❖ *See, sense and feel that your physical, emotional body and mental body are the same; they have the same color; the Color of God. They are in harmony.*

❖ *Breathe out once.*

❖ *See, sense and feel that you are infinite. Time does not exist. Bring the infinity sign inside you and expand yourself with this sign all over the Universe. Feel that you are the infinite spirit, the Mother. See, sense and feel everything and all in the Universe.*

❖ *Breathe out once and open your eyes.*

❖ *Write down your experience.*

The Green Field Exercise

❖ *Move into the Heart (see <u>Moving into the Heart</u>).*

❖ *Breathe out once (let out a long, slow exhalation through your mouth).*

❖ *See, sense and feel the taste of lemon in your mouth. Associate lemon with either your emotional or your mental body. Now feel the taste of honey in your mouth, associate it with the other body. Now mix them together. How do you feel?*

❖ *Breathe out once.*

❖ *See, sense and feel that you are walking through a green field together with all of your friends. Try to see, sense and feel the direction you are walking in: north, east, south or west. Where is the sun?*

❖ *Breathe out once.*

❖ *See, sense and feel now that the green grass field is inside you. How do you feel? In that same green field, realize that you are alone. How do you feel now? Again feel that the green grass is inside you.*

If you feel sad and lonely, bring your friends back; otherwise, if you feel detached, continue walking alone.

❖ *See, sense and feel that we are all one. Look inside and see the green field and realize that it is empty; you are the green field now.*

❖ *Breathe out once and open your eyes.*

❖ *Write down your experience.*

The Great Masters Exercise

❖ *Move into the Heart (see <u>Moving into the Heart</u>).*

❖ *Breathe out once (let out a long, slow exhalation through your mouth).*

❖ *See, sense and feel that you were alive more than 2000 years ago. You are in a crowd watching Jesus speak. You are one of his disciples. He is giving you a lesson about unconditional love and he is behaving towards your neighbor in the same manner you would behave towards yourself. Listen to what Jesus has to say and allow all the feelings that arise in you to settle within you; accept yourself and feel love for yourself.*

❖ *Breathe out once.*

❖ *See, sense and feel that you are sitting in a lotus posture in front of Buddha over 2500 years ago. You are one of his disciples. He is giving you a lesson about compassion and understanding people around you. Listen to Buddha and allow all the feelings that arise in you to settle within you.*

❖ *Breathe out once.*

❖ *See, sense and feel that you are a Master; there are people around you. You are sending them love and energy and you are teaching them a lesson about innocence. You are telling them that they have no enemy other than themselves and teach them to beware of the temptation to perceive themselves as being unfairly treated. Teach them that innocence cannot be obtained by handing out guilt to someone else.*

❖ *Breathe out once and open your eyes.*

❖ *Write down your experience.*

The Most Familiar Place Exercise

- ❖ *Move into the Heart (see <u>Moving into the Heart</u>).*
- ❖ *Breathe out once (let out a long, slow exhalation through your mouth).*
- ❖ *See, sense and feel that you are in the middle of your most familiar and favorite room of your childhood. Start cleaning the room, from right to the left. Take a vacuum cleaner and clean the room, the bed, the floor, the desk. Now push everything, including all the furniture, out of the room to the left.*
- ❖ *Breathe out once.*
- ❖ *See, sense and feel that you are in the middle of your most familiar and favorite place in nature. Start cleaning the place; the grass or the tree or the lake water or the sky. Push all pollution and radiation to the left until it is all clean.*
- ❖ *See, sense and feel that you are in the middle of your most familiar and favorite place in the Universe; it might be a star, a planet, a galaxy. Try to feel the energy there and relax. Just enjoy the place.*
- ❖ *Breathe out once and open your eyes.*
- ❖ *Write down your experience.*

The Ocean Masters Exercise

- ❖ *Move into the Heart (see <u>Moving into the Heart</u>).*
- ❖ *Breathe out once (let out a long, slow exhalation through your mouth).*
- ❖ *See, sense and feel that you are meditating on a beautiful white sandy beach near the beautiful blue and crystal clear ocean; you can hear the pleasant sound of the waves and a soft breeze is gently touching your face.*
- ❖ *Hear the call of the Dolphins and the Whales; this call is vibrating in your heart.*
- ❖ *Get up and go into the water. Start swimming into the ocean; the dolphins and whales are coming and taking you to the middle of*

the ocean. Meditate there with their Master Dolphin and Master Whale who are waiting for you.

❖ *The Master Dolphin has a message for you. Hear this message. He has a gift for you too; take the gift.*

❖ *The Master Whale has a message for you. Hear this message. She has a gift for you too.*

❖ *Now take the gifts with you and continue swimming back to the shore.*

❖ *Go back to the white sandy beach and put the gifts down in front of you; the gifts transform in something else; what are they now?*

❖ *Now, there on the beach, close your eyes and meditate on the message given to you by the Master Dolphin and Master Whale.*

❖ *Breathe out once and open your eyes.*

❖ *Write down your experience.*

The Healing Exercise

❖ *Move into the Heart (see <u>Moving into the Heart</u>).*

❖ *Breathe out once (let out a long, slow exhalation through your mouth).*

❖ *See, sense and feel that healing has been accomplished in the moment when you no longer see any value in pain; do that now and clear the idea of pain out of you.*

❖ *See, sense and feel that any area of pain in your body has healed instantly. See that pain is of no value and suffering is futile; it is useless.*

❖ *Breathe out once.*

❖ *See and sense that the whole humanity feels the same way as you do now: the pain and suffering vanish out of each person on this planet.*

❖ *Breathe out once and open your eyes.*

❖ *Write down your experience.*

The Breathing Exercise

❖ *Move into the Heart (see <u>Moving into the Heart</u>).*

❖ *Breathe out once (let out a long, slow exhalation through your mouth).*

❖ *See, sense and feel that your body is part of the universe; everything in the body is part of the universe.*

❖ *See, sense and feel that your breath is a bridge between your body and the universe; one end of this bridge is in your body, while the other is outside in nothingness.*

❖ *Breathe out once.*

❖ *See, sense and feel that you know half of the bridge that is inside your body, but you do not know the other half of the bridge; where does your breath go?*

❖ *See, sense and feel that if you were to know the other half of the bridge, you would suddenly know nothingness; you would be transformed and know the other dimension. Try to sense where your breath goes; see the nothingness.*

❖ *See, sense and feel that if you were to stop your breath, you would stop your mind. Your breath and your mind are inter-related; stop your breath for three seconds and realize that your mind has stopped too.*

❖ *Breathe out once and open your eyes.*

❖ *Write down your experience.*

The Creation Exercise

❖ *Move into the Heart (see <u>Moving into the Heart</u>).*

❖ *Breathe out once (let out a long, slow exhalation through your mouth).*

❖ *See, sense and feel that anything you create inside the heart is of much greater value than what you create inside your brain.*

❖ *See an image now of a creation from your heart: feel the vibration of this creation. See, sense and feel the energy coming from this* image; a unity field is surrounding this creation and you feel safe and protected.

- ❖ Now see an image of a creation from your brain; feel the vibration of this creation.
- ❖ Breathe out once.
- ❖ See, sense and feel how the world would be if all humanity created only from the heart.
- ❖ Breathe out once and open your eyes.
- ❖ Write down your experience.

The Inner Light Exercise

- ❖ Move into the Heart (see <u>Moving into the Heart</u>).
- ❖ Breathe out once (let out a long, slow exhalation through your mouth).
- ❖ See, sense and feel that there is a light in you that the world cannot recognize; open your eyes within and see this light. Realize that if you use the eyes of the world you will not see the light within; you need to use your inner vision, your inner eyes.
- ❖ See, sense and feel that this inner light is a reflection of God's love and light.
- ❖ Breathe out once.
- ❖ See, sense and feel that your inner light is projecting outwards and you can see the world shining in innocence and blessed with divine clarity and love.
- ❖ See, sense and feel that the inner light is keeping you safe from every form of danger and pain.
- ❖ Breathe out once.
- ❖ See, sense and feel how all people see their inner light and that all people's minds have been restored and re-established completely with this love and light.
- ❖ Breathe out once and open your eyes.
- ❖ Write down your experience.

The Love of God Exercise

- ❖ *Move into the Heart (see <u>Moving into the Heart</u>).*
- ❖ *Breathe out once (let out a long, slow exhalation through your mouth).*
- ❖ *See, sense and feel that the love of God is everywhere: you can see it, smell it, touch it and feel it all around you. The love of God is like an ocean and you are living in this ocean.*
- ❖ *Breathe out once.*
- ❖ *See, sense and feel that what is not love, is always fear and nothing else.*
- ❖ *See, sense and feel that confusing sacrificing for love is so deep, that you are unable to perceive love without sacrifice; see that this sacrifice is fear, not love.*
- ❖ *See, sense and feel that you have the gift of freedom; you do not need to sacrifice anything. See that you are completely free. Feel the Love of God within you and around you.*
- ❖ *Breathe out once and open your eyes.*
- ❖ *Write down your experience.*

The Teachers of God Exercise

- ❖ *Move into the Heart (see <u>Moving into the Heart</u>).*
- ❖ *Breathe out once (let out a long, slow exhalation through your mouth).*
- ❖ *See, sense and feel that atonement and reconciliation correct illusions, not truth; truth does not need to be corrected.*
- ❖ *See, sense and feel that there is a group of teachers that have a special role in the reconciliation plan; the Teachers of God.*
- ❖ *See, sense and feel the nine characteristics of the advanced Teachers of God: open-mindedness, generosity, patience, tolerance, joy, gentleness, honesty, trust and unconditional love.*
- ❖ *Breathe out once.*
- ❖ *See, sense and feel that the main function of the Teachers of God is to bring true learning to the world; their function is to unlearn what we think is true, what we think is real and to teach true learning.*

❖ *See, sense and feel that part of their function is to give complete forgiveness to the world; to teach how we have to let go of all things that prevent forgiveness.*

❖ *Breathe out once.*

❖ *See, sense and feel that you are one of the Teachers of God; see which of the nine characteristics of the advanced Teachers of God are mirrored in yourself now (open-mindedness, generosity, patience, tolerance, joy, gentleness, honesty, trust and unconditional love).*

❖ *Breathe out once and open your eyes.*

❖ *Write down your experience.*

The Goal of Truth Exercise

❖ *Move into the Heart (see <u>Moving into the Heart</u>).*

❖ *Breathe out once (let out a long, slow exhalation through your mouth).*

❖ *See, sense and feel that whenever you are uncertain in your life, you need a clarification of your goal. The heart will give you your goal; see, sense and feel your goal here on this world. Call it the goal of truth (two minutes). When you see, sense and feel your goal of truth you will experience peace; a divine peace.*

❖ *See, sense and feel that the only characteristics required by the goal of truth are faith and trust.*

❖ *Breathe out once.*

❖ *See, sense and feel that what you want to happen simply constitutes a situation as a means to achieve your goal of truth.*

❖ *See now how many situations in your life were in accordance with your goal of truth; understand that your life is fragmented and it is not in unity, because you do not have a goal of truth.*

❖ *Remember your goal of truth and use it whenever you feel conflict and fragmentation around you.*

❖ *Breathe out once and open your eyes.*

❖ *Write down your experience.*

The Master Initiation Exercise

❖ *Move into the Heart (see <u>Moving into the Heart</u>).*

❖ *Breathe out once (let out a long, slow exhalation through your mouth).*

❖ *See, sense and feel that you are in front of your Master and feel that he is helping you to awaken; stop fighting with yourself and open the door of your heart. Do not close up. Do not be afraid.*

❖ *See, sense and feel that you are vulnerable; the Master can enter you. You are humble, surrendered and open to receive.*

❖ *Breathe out once.*

❖ *See, sense and feel that, in order to be initiated, you must surrender yourself totally and let the energy flow down from the Master to you; this energy flows down from the Master to anyone who is receptive, humble and surrendered.*

❖ *See, sense and feel that you are a valley and the Master is a peak of a mountain; see a deep transfer of energy from the Master to you, just like the water flows from the peak of the mountain down to the beautiful valley. Let the purest energy come to you; you have a receptive attitude, a deep humbleness and you start to receive energy and knowledge from the Master (2 minutes).*

❖ *See, sense and feel that initiation is a transfer of inner energy and if you are open and receptive, the Master can enter your heart and transform you, clean you and clear your mind.*

❖ *Breathe out once.*

❖ *See, sense and feel that humanity cannot be initiated; it cannot be awakened, because it does not trust and it sets conditions.*

❖ *See, sense and feel that once humanity opens its heart, the Masters can help it and it can awaken, just as you did.*

❖ *Breathe out once and open your eyes.*

❖ *Write down your experience.*

The Sounds of God Exercise

❖ *Move into the Heart (see <u>Moving into the Heart</u>).*

❖ *Breathe out once (let out a long, slow exhalation through your mouth).*

❖ *See, sense and feel that your Master is giving you a sound that resonates with your energy; this sound is a key that unlocks the energy of your heart.*

❖ *Start chanting this sound inside your heart and see, sense and feel that this entire energy has begun to move around you like a rainbow of colors and sounds (one minute).*

❖ *Remember that this mantra is your personal sound and it belongs only to you; it cannot be given to anyone else and you promise your Master to keep it just for you.*

❖ *Breathe out once.*

❖ *See, sense and feel that life everywhere has a deep, energetic sound inside that unlocks the energy around; any flower, any tree, and animal, any element: water, fire, wind. Listen to these sounds and let them fill your heart.*

❖ *See, sense and feel the sound of Mother Earth; let it fill your heart too.*

❖ *See, sense and feel the sound of Father Sun and realize that all around us is a giant symphony of God' sounds.*

❖ *Breathe out once.*

❖ *See, sense and feel that the Universe is chanting the sound AUM. Feel each letter sound: first the 'A', then the "U' and finally the 'M" and let them enter your heart.*

❖ *Breathe out once and open your eyes.*

❖ *Write down your experience.*

The Universal Unity Exercise

- ❖ *Move into the Heart (see <u>Moving into the Heart</u>).*
- ❖ *Breathe out once (let out a long, slow exhalation through your mouth).*
- ❖ *See, sense and feel that God is unity; even if you live in a material and physical world. See, sense and feel the unity of the Universe; how do you perceive the unity of the Universe?*
- ❖ *Next, see, sense and feel that you are part of this unity. How do you feel?*
- ❖ *Breathe out once.*
- ❖ *See, sense and feel the Isle of Light in the middle of the Universe where The Unqualified Absolute upholds the physical universe.*
- ❖ *See, sense and feel that the Isle of Light is the actual source of all material universes: past, present and future.*
- ❖ *See, sense and feel that every impulse of every electron of your body, thought or spirit is an acting unit in the whole Universe.*
- ❖ *Breathe out once and open your eyes.*
- ❖ *Write down your experience.*

The Acceptance Exercise

- ❖ *Move into the Heart (see <u>Moving into the Heart</u>).*
- ❖ *Breathe out once (let out a long, slow exhalation through your mouth).*
- ❖ *See, sense and feel that life is divided into two aspects: one is the seen world and the other is the unseen, the hidden manifestation of the world. Realize that there is no contradiction between those two aspects and they are just two aspects of the same existence.*
- ❖ *See, sense and feel that, because you cannot see the whole, the world appears to be something which is against divinity and you have to fight the world to reach the divine aspect within.*
- ❖ *See, sense and feel that the whole is whole and the part that you see is the world and the part that is hidden is the divine, or God. This*

part, however, is here and now. You do not need to travel to find it; you only need to open your eyes and see it; you only need to awaken.

❖ *See, sense and feel that if you do not accept the world totally, then you are tense and divided, in conflict and fear.*

❖ *See, sense and feel that you do not need to be in favor of the world or against the world; you only need to accept it as it is. Do that now: accept the world as it is and you will be instantly transformed. You will see, sense and feel the unseen part, the divinity. All your energy will be relieved and not engaged in conflicts anymore.*

❖ *Accept your fate, whatever it is and let yourself flow like a river and change, just as the water flows down to the ocean.*

❖ *Breathe out once and open your eyes.*

❖ *Write down your experience.*

The Trinity Exercise

❖ *Move into the Heart (see <u>Moving into the Heart</u>).*

❖ *Breathe out once (let out a long, slow exhalation through your mouth).*

❖ *See, sense and feel the three personalizations of God: the Universal Father, the Eternal Son and the Infinite Spirit. Realize that on sub-infinite levels there are three Absolutes, but in infinity they appear to be ONE.*

❖ *See, sense and feel the three characteristics of each being of the Universe: truth, beauty and goodness. Then see, sense and feel that these characteristics are bringing you closer to God; they are helping you perceive God in your mind, matter and spirit.*

❖ *Finally see, sense and feel that, for you, truth, beauty and goodness embrace the full revelation of divinity reality.*

❖ *Breathe out once.*

❖ *See, sense and feel what Jesus explained to the twelve Apostles around him when he said: "He who would be greatest among you, let him become server of all". Further see, sense and feel why it is that, when you become the highest level of consciousness and you are like a light, you need to help others who are lost in darkness.*

❖ *See, sense and feel that love is desire to do good onto others.*
❖ *See, sense and feel how many times in your life you did good onto others and realized that you created love when you did all these acts.*
❖ *Breathe out once and open your eyes.*
❖ *Write down your experience.*

Practical exercises that can be used in our daily activities with or without doing a meditation

Reviewing your Life's Best Moments Meditation

Use your favorite music meditation for this exercise; a song that keeps you in alpha waves.

❖ *Move into the Heart (see <u>Moving into the Heart</u>).*
❖ *Breathe out once (let out a long, slow exhalation through your mouth).*
❖ *See yourself as you are today, now, in this moment.*
❖ *Rewind your life from this moment back to the moment when you were born and see, sense and feel your life's best moments.*
❖ *Try not to be attached to it; just see it again as if you are watching a movie and observe how you were at that moment.*
❖ *How do you feel now that you have seen your life's best moments?*
❖ *Practice this exercise once a week to recharge your energy.*

God's Unity Consciousness Exercise

Practical Exercise to dissolve yourself into God's Unity Consciousness.
      Inhale into the Heart; open the heart and feel the prana entering your physical heart.
      This is a very good exercise to connect with your inner essence and feel God within.

This is to be practiced whenever you feel like it, but at least 5 minutes before falling asleep. It will help you dream consciously after a few weeks of practicing.

Forgiveness Meditation

❖ *Use your favorite music meditation for this exercise; a song that keeps you in alpha waves.*

❖ *Move into the Heart (see Moving into the Heart).*

❖ *Breathe out once (let out a long, slow exhalation through your mouth).*

❖ *Now, bring into your heart the image and energy of those with whom you had an issue or a conflict and remember that we are all the same. If the Creator made you, then the Creator has also certainly made the people with whom you were in conflict.*

Practice forgiveness and understanding; whenever you bring a person into your heart, look into the eyes of that person and say to him or her: "I forgive you [the name of person]"; after this step, see that you are in your heart and say to yourself: "I forgive myself".

Remember that a conflict is always duality and as much as we want to believe that fault lies with others, there are karmic links from this life or past lives that connect us deeply with these persons. Therefore, you need to forgive yourself too.

Union with God through Prayer (Divine Prayer)

❖ *Move into the Heart (see Moving into the Heart).*

❖ *Allow any prayer that comes to you in a natural way to manifest in your heart and say that prayer there in your Heart.*

❖ *See, sense, feel and know that the Prayer is heard by God.*

The Three Centers Cleaning Meditation

❖ *Move into the Heart (see <u>Moving into the Heart</u>).*

❖ *Shift your attention behind your navel where the center of the first sphere of our body is: the center of being.*

❖ *Breathe in there as if you are filling a bottle with water.*

❖ *In a conscious way, bring prana there and see the sphere filled with prana.*

❖ *There are ten rays of light leading outwards from the center of the first sphere, touching the circumference of the sphere, the sphere's margin.*

❖ *Turn your attention to the sphere of the heart: the second sphere of your body where you have your feeling center.*

❖ *Breathe in there, as if you are filling a bottle with water.*

❖ *In a conscious way, bring prana there and see the sphere filled with prana.*

❖ *There are ten rays of light going outwards from the center of the sphere of the heart, touching the circumference of the sphere, the sphere's margin.*

❖ *Turn your attention now to the third sphere; the knowledge sphere: the sphere of the third eye that is up in the middle of your brain on a straight line from your forehead.*

❖ *See, sense and feel your third eye right in the middle of the forehead and focus on it.*

❖ *Now turn your breath flow from your heart center to the middle of your brain and feel that your head is filled with prana, with light.*

❖ *There are eight rays of light going outwards from the center of the sphere of the head, touching the circumference of the sphere, the sphere's margin.*

❖ *See, sense and feel that all your three spheres are filled with light and prana.*

❖ *Practice this meditation once a week or as many times as possible: it helps center yourself.*

The Gratitude Exercise

❖ *Move into the Heart (see <u>Moving into the Heart</u>).*

❖ *See, sense and feel the word "Gratitude" in front of you, written in words made of pure golden light; what do you experience when you see these words in front of you?*

❖ *Once a month and for three days, see the word "Gratitude" in front of you before doing an activity; any activity, even walking or eating.*

❖ *See, sense and feel gratitude for each step you take, each piece of bread or slice of apple you eat, each word you say and hear.*

❖ *Feel the unconditional love behind each activity, fill your heart and soul with it and let it stay there.*

Before falling asleep, feel gratitude for the day that has passed and, in the morning, feel gratitude that you are starting a new day.

Empty your Mind Exercise

❖ *Move into the Heart (see <u>Moving into the Heart</u>).*

❖ *See, sense and feel that your mind is a blue sky and your thoughts are white clouds gently moving in it.*

❖ *With your intention, move the thoughts with a soft wind; the wind is gently blowing from left to right.*

Another Way of Looking at the World Exercise

To be practiced for two days in row.

First Day (three sessions of 30 minutes)

This exercise explains why you can see all purpose in everything. Move into the Heart every morning before you start your day. This exercise tells us that God is in everything we see and feel.

So, for 30 minutes, three times a day, begin by repeating the idea and applying it on randomly chosen subjects, naming each one specifically and clearly. You can begin with what you see around you:

God is in this tree.
God is in this computer.
God is in this door.
God is in this apple.
God is in this person (say the name of the person).
If you focus and do this without thinking of something else, you should feel peace and very calm and have the sense that we are all one.

Second Day *(three sessions of 30 minutes)*
This exercise continues the idea from the previous exercise and adds another dimension to it.
Move into the Heart every morning before you start your day.
This exercise tells us that God is the light in which we see and feel everything.
So, again for 30 minutes, three times a day, begin by repeating the idea and applying it on randomly chosen subjects:
God is the light in which I see this tree.
God is the light in which I see this computer.
God is the light in which I see this apple.
God is the light in which I see this person.
If you have a chance during the day, close your eyes a couple of times and repeat to yourself: "God is the light in which I see and feel everything". If you focus and do this without thinking of something else, you should feel peace and very calm and have the sense that we are all made of LIGHT.

Moving into the Heart Exercise

❖ *Close your eyes.*
❖ *Breathe three times (draw in a normal breath and let out a long, slow exhalation through the mouth. As you do this, see all your problems, issues, concerns and internal conflicts going out and away); then breathe in and out normally.*

❖ *Imagine a spiral staircase going down from the middle of your brain to the middle of your chest.*

❖ *Go down the stairs.*

❖ *Step off the stairs and slowly turn to your left.*

❖ *There is a door there that goes into your heart (it can be any type of door you can imagine).*

❖ *Open the door and step inside your heart; remember to close the door behind you.*

❖ *For a moment see, sense and feel the power and love emanating from your heart.*

PART FIVE

Index of Heart Imagery
Meditations and Exercises

"Because truth is not linear, but global, and not successive,
but simultaneous, it can therefore not be expressed in words:
it must be lived."

Rumi, D 17925

Index of Meditations and Exercises

Introduction to the History of Heart Imagery

The Heart: Coordinator of our Body's Energies

The Purpose of Life

The Seven Ancient Heart Imagery Exercises

Union with God

We Need Clarity

ABOUT THE AUTHOR

Following the exceptional feedback received for the book *This Now Is Eternity*, Daniel continues his dialogue with the Great Masters, bringing even more valuable information and exercises to the whole of humanity.

Daniel is a world traveling Master helping people understand their intimate connection with their Inner Selves and God. He is the first person in the world (in modern times) to explain and define the origin of the ancient Heart Imagery system. Heart Imagery originates from the ancient Tibetan, Sumerian and Vedic spiritual mystery schools that are related to the highest number of Mystery Schools: 555.

He began teaching teach Zen Meditation in 1981 and practiced the "spinal breathing" meditation between 1981 and 1992; later on he discovered that, in fact, he was practicing Kriya Pranayama of Great Master Babaji's Kriya Yoga.

Since 1996, he has been teaching Meditation Day Workshops and Heart Imagery Workshops worldwide.

Having spent a few years in meditation in north of Tibet, Daniel created "*The School of the Heart*" in 1999. Ten years later he created "*The School of Meditation*" in Toronto.

As an international lecturer and Martial Arts Master (Tai Chi Master and Karate Traditional Black Belt 5 DAN in WJKA – World Japan Karate Association), Daniel is dedicated to inspiring the world to shift from violence to peace and from anger to love. Through his work, workshops and spiritual conferences, Daniel has changed the lives of thousands of people.

Following his practice under the Tibetan Great Lama Masters, Daniel worked with a group of well known Masters from different schools of meditation (Osho, Dalai Lama, Babaji, Lahiri Mahasaya, Sri Yukteswar, Paramahansa Yogananda, Paramahansa Hariharananda, Paramahansa Prajnananda, Ana Pricop, Di Yu Ming, Sadhguru, Drunvalo Melchizedek, Anastasia) who train their students to be in the Heart.

Now, together with his own workshops (*Meditation Day, Kriya Yoga* and *Heart Imagery*), Daniel also brings the *Awakening the Illuminated Heart* workshop to the world.

With these spiritual seminars, Daniel shares a message of hope and possibility to anyone who wishes to experience a new understanding of life; an understanding which comes from the heart.

Daniel had the opportunity to work with Indigo Children from all over the world. He is blessed to work with children, teaching them Tai Chi and Meditation.

Having being interviewed all over the world and constantly invited to write articles in magazines and on-line publications (Spirit of Ma'at, Collective Evolution, Vision, etc.), Daniel is one of the most prominent Masters of Meditations known worldwide, showing the inner power that one can achieve using the Heart''s unconditional love.

For more information visit *www.danielmitel.com* and *www. heartimagery.org*.

In order to help Daniel continue his journey all over
the world, please consider contributing a donation
by visiting the Donations page at his website.
Daniel has made generous donations all over the world
to orphanages, homeless shelters, animal shelters and
organizations dealing with cleaning the environment.

PRAISE for HEART IMAGERY

"...Heart Imagery – is an alchemical work, that unites ancient tradition of imagery with new evolutionary energy unfolding on our planet. This work is profoundly healing and at the same time can be done by anyone, no matter how one is evolved in spiritual area. The way how Daniel guides you through the exercises is really a master work, he observes your progress and help you to overcome your inner obstacles that come up. I would advice this workshop to anyone who is ready to let go of old stuff, heal himself and open new wonderful doors of joy and growth. With love and gratitude..."
Mariam

"...I attended some really well done seminars (Tom Kenyon, Neale Walsch, Catherine Shainberg and Eric Pearl) but I can say that Heart Imagery series are by far the most powerful workshops in the world. This knowledge is foundation of all spiritual schools! Daniel is, undoubtedly, one of the Masters of today' spiritual world. In light..."
Irina

"...Having attended the 1st day of Heart Imagery in Athens… I am flabbergasted. Having taken in the past so many courses on deprogramming the mind and access the Heart, having read so many books from various sources, contemporary and traditional, I had never encountered such powerful tools that have immediate effect, such as those given to us today by Daniel Mitel. Now it's totally up to each of us to take responsibility of our selves and have the intention to follow these exercises through. And this is only the beginning..."

Demetra Teresa – Athens

DANIEL MITEL'S WEBSITES

www.danielmitel.com
www.heartimagery.org

WORKSHOPS by DANIEL MITEL
AVAILABLE WORLD-WIDE

Kriya Yoga
http://danielmitel.com/yogananda-and-kriya-yoga-masters/

Heart Imagery:
Cleaning the Past and Self-Renewal
Healing and Emotional Clarity
Union with God
http://danielmitel.com/heart-imagery/
http://heartimagery.org/

Awakening the Illuminated Heart
http://danielmitel.com/awakwening-the-illuminated-heart-atih-workshop-schedule/

Printed in the United States
By Bookmasters